HOW TO READ YOUR OPPONENT'S CARDS

The Bridge Experts' Way to Locate Missing High Cards

by Mike Lawrence
of the World Champion Aces

♠　♡　◇　♣

**Published by
Devyn Press, Inc.
Louisville, Kentucky**

Cover by Bonnie Baron Pollack

Printed in the United States of America.

Devyn Press, Inc.
3600 Chamberlain Lane, Suite 230
Louisville, KY 40241

ISBN 0-910791-48-1

Foreword

When Mike Lawrence became a World Bridge Champion at the age of 30, he was the second youngest player ever to achieve that rank. When his team successfully defended that title in 1971, he set a record as the youngest player ever to have won the Bermuda Bowl twice. Now, as he is preparing to make it three straight wins, he remains the youngest star of America's famous Aces, the team organized by Ira Corn for the express purpose of winning back the World Championship; the team that succeeded in bringing the Bermuda Bowl back to this side of the Atlantic for the first time in sixteen years.

This is Mike's first book—not very strange, since he is only 32. What *is* remarkable is that, having undertaken to explain the most difficult art in the game of contract bridge, he has succeeded to such an extent that any reader who can follow suit can also follow the process by which the experts take guessing out of their play; the logic by which they *know* who's got the queen of spades instead of trying to guess.

Mike Lawrence is a young man many people have characterized as "difficult to get to know. He always seems to be thinking about something." The truth is, he usually *is* thinking about something. And when he plays bridge, he is thinking about the right things.

What he has done in this book is to tell you what to think about, why, and how. Dozens of able writers and brilliant players have tried to explain the process called "card reading." Mike Lawrence has hit upon a way to lead you along the road to a place where suddenly a great light dawns, the path ahead is clear, and the "secret" is revealed so that every reader can learn the answer.

What's more, in the process of doing so, he has produced a book that any bridge buff will find totally absorbing—a challenge that equals the challenge of the game itself.

RICHARD L. FREY

Introduction
A Salute from the Captain

Mike Lawrence is not only a phenomenal bridge player but, even more rare, a phenomenal *young* bridge player. He began establishing his status as one of the great future players in the United States when he began winning major events at the age of 21. Bridge is one of those rare competitive sports where many top-notch players are in their 40's and 50's; practically no bridge player ever makes it before the age of 30. For example, B.J. Becker won the right to represent the United States in 1973 international play at the slightly young age of 69.

One of the reasons for Mike Lawrence's preeminence as a bridge player is reflected in this book which deals with the "delicate interpretation of delicate data" at the bridge table. We call it DIDD. This involves information that is given in the bidding as well as information that can be deduced by what was *not* bid and the interpretation of pauses and hesitations and speed of play by opponents—the art of "table presence." It involves guesswork based on logic stemming from each card as it is played, thus reaffirming or pointing to new directions of logic for the likelihood of where the remaining unplayed cards are located.

Of course, all high-level bridge players have to be very capable in this special area of expertise, but it is where Mike Lawrence excels. It is valuable not only when you are playing the hand but also when you are defending.

In the hand following, Mike, as East, is defending against a contract of 4 Spades.

Vulnerable: North-South

Dealer: West

NORTH
♠ A J 2
♡ 10 8 4
◇ Q 10 8
♣ A 10 3 2

WEST
♠ 4
♡ 5 2
◇ A 7 6 4 2
♣ 9 8 7 5 4

EAST
♠ K 10 8 5
♡ K J 9 6 3
◇ K J 5
♣ 6

SOUTH
♠ Q 9 7 6 3
♡ A Q 7
◇ 9 3
♣ K Q J

The bidding:

WEST	NORTH	EAST	SOUTH
Pass	Pass	1 ♡	1 ♠
Pass	3 ♠	Pass	4 ♠
Pass	Pass	Pass	

Opening lead: Heart five.

The bidding was aggressive. However, the vulnerable game contract was very reasonable, since the only danger lay in the possible loss of two trump tricks.

West led the heart five and East's nine was taken by declarer's queen. A spade was led to dummy's jack and held the trick! Lawrence not only refused the trick, he false-carded with the eight.

Observe the course of play had Lawrence taken the king. A heart continuation would have been won and a spade led to dummy's ace. West's discard would reveal the trump situation and East's trump ten would be finessed. One of declarer's red suit losers would be discarded on the long club and the contract would have been scored.

Lawrence's play gave declarer room for thought. If the eight were a singleton, then the play of the trump ace and another would lose two trump tricks and the contract. Declarer could guard against this by coming back to his hand and pushing the queen through. Then, if East had started with 10-8 doubleton, an overtrick could be made, "blotting" the ten while repeating the apparently successful finesse.

Declarer went for the "safety play" and lost the hand. The defense scored two spade tricks, two diamonds and a heart to defeat the contract two tricks.

Should declarer have disregarded the trump eight and played for the actual holding? A tough question. The main point is that had Lawrence *not* played deceptively, declarer would not have had any problem to solve.

Another remarkable hand where Mike made a series of winning decisions took place in an inter-city match between Houston and The Aces, representing Dallas. Mike was sitting South.

Vulnerable: East-West

Dealer: North

                    NORTH
                    ♠ Q 4
                    ♡ 8 6 3 2
                    ◊ A J 2
                    ♣ A 9 7 5
WEST   EAST
♠ 10 7 6 3   ♠ A J 9 5
♡ 7 5   ♡ K Q
◊ K Q 6 4   ◊ 10 8 7 5
♣ K J 3   ♣ Q 8 6
                    SOUTH
                    ♠ K 8 2
                    ♡ A J 10 9 4
                    ◊ 9 3
                    ♣ 10 4 2

The bidding:

NORTH	EAST	SOUTH	WEST
Pass	Pass	2 ♡	Pass
Pass	Double	Pass	2 ♠
3 ♡	Pass	Pass	Pass

Opening lead: Spade three.

The spade lead was ducked in dummy, East playing the jack and South winning the king. Not wishing to use dummy's entries to finesse twice in the trump suit, South played the ace and another heart. East won the heart king, cashed his spade ace and led another spade, forcing dummy to ruff. The position was:

```
                      NORTH
                      ♠  —
                      ♡  8
                      ◇  A J 2
                      ♣  A 9 7 5
WEST                                    EAST
♠  7                                    ♠  9
♡  —                                    ♡  —
◇  K Q 6 4                              ◇  10 8 7 5
♣  K J 3                                ♣  Q 8 6
                      SOUTH
                      ♠  —
                      ♡  10 9 4
                      ◇  9 3
                      ♣  10 4 2
```

At this point, Mike Lawrence had a strong feeling about the location of the outstanding high cards. East had already shown 10 points in the major suits and was sure to have one of the club honors, as West certainly would have led clubs with an original holding of K-Q-J.

East had passed originally, so he was unlikely to hold more than 12 points. Thus West was clearly in possession of both missing diamond face cards. Locating the high cards, however, solved only half the problem. Finding a way to take advantage of the knowledge still remained to be accomplished.

Declarer could not use his trump entry to play a diamond toward dummy, since he could not return to his hand safely to repeat the play. So Lawrence led a low club from dummy.

Whichever defender won the trick, he had to play a minor suit. If clubs were continued, the fourth club would become established for a diamond discard. If a diamond were returned, Lawrence would allow West to win the king or queen and then return to his hand with a trump to finesse against the remaining diamond honor.

An unusual solution to an unusual problem. One well worth remembering.

You can see why the Aces are indeed proud of Mike Lawrence as a great bridge player and as a member of The Aces World Championship Team which brought the Bermuda Bowl back to the United States in 1970 after a sixteen-year absence.

IRA G. CORN, JR.
Captain of the World Champion Aces

Contents

I

Sizing Up the Case

♠ ♡ ◇ ♣

This book is not going to be another oration on bridge technique. Terms such as safety plays, squeezes, endplays, and coups will have little or no place here, and any references to them will be in name only. What will be discussed are the thought processes of the good player as he is proceeding through a hand that requires one correct guess for success, or perhaps a series of correct guesses.

If you have ever watched the play of someone who has a firm understanding of the ideas presented in this book, at the end of a hand you may have asked such questions as:

"What made you play East instead of West for the queen of spades?"

"How did you know the king of hearts was singleton?"

"Why did you finesse the diamonds instead of the clubs?"

The answers to these questions come from applying the rules of card placing or card locating, and this book intends to give you guidelines for determining who has which cards. When you know where the cards are, it will be much easier to apply the aforementioned bridge techniques.

This chapter will take a brief look at some hands, and will discuss them from two points of view:

(1) No information is available, *i.e.*, no bidding and a noninformative lead.

(2) There has been a helpful auction, or the opening lead gives some information.

Frequently throughout this book questions will be asked. Attempt to answer them before going on. Learning is always a process of observing and *doing*. The questions will be real-life situations, and you should take the time to answer them, for they will approximate actual conditions at the bridge table.

1

Always note the information given. Try to make this a habit, so that it is not necessary to refer back. Look at the auction when given, note the opening lead, who has shown up with what card or cards, etc.

Opening leads in this book are standard. The defenders will lead the king from sequences headed by the ace-king or the king-queen. The ace is led from the ace-king doubleton, or when leading partner's suit. The queen is led from sequences headed by the queen-jack, or it may be a doubleton or a singleton. In real life, as in this book, most of your opponents will use standard leads, for it is more important for the defenders to try to give each other information early in the play than to try to deceive the declarer.

You are in three notrump:

NORTH
♠ Q 10 7
♡ A K 2
♢ J 10 5 4
♣ 10 3 2

SOUTH
♠ 9 8 3
♡ Q J 4
♢ A K Q 3
♣ A J 4

How would you play three notrump in these three cases?

(1) East-West did not bid, and West leads a heart.
(2) East-West did not bid, and West leads and wins the spade king and then shifts to a heart.
(3) West opened the bidding with one club and then leads a heart.

Answers:

(1) With no clues to go on, your best play for your ninth trick would be to lead the spade nine and finesse against West's hoped-for jack.

(2) West's lead of the spade king tells you that he holds the spade ace as well. This time you should lead a spade to the queen.

(3) Your side has 27 points in high cards. The opponents have 13. If West truly has an opening bid he will have the ace and king of spades. Unless you feel he is fooling around with his opening bid, you should lead toward the spade queen. It would be wrong to play to the spade ten, as it is just barely possible that East holds the jack.

In these examples you were simply given different information which gave you reasons to approach the play of the same hand in different ways. It is almost as though you had to solve three different problems, even though at first sight they seemed to be the same.

A look at a few more hands may help to give you a feel for this approach. This time you are in four hearts.

```
NORTH
♠  K Q 9 3
♡  8 6 3
◇  A 7 6
♣  Q 5 2


SOUTH
♠  8 6 2
♡  A K Q J 10 4
◇  K 10
♣  8 4
```

How would you play this hand under these varying conditions?

(1) No opposing bidding. West leads the trump nine.
(2) East opens one club. West leads the ace of clubs and continues with the three of clubs. You trump the third club, with West following suit.
(3) No opposing bidding. West leads the spade jack. Dummy's king wins the first trick.

Answers:

(1) With no clues, you should just lead spades toward the dummy twice. Hope West has the ace of spades.

(2) If, after East's opening bid, you believe he has the ace of spades, then you should finesse the nine on the first round of spades. If you play the king or queen, East will win and you will have a sure spade loser remaining.

(3) West's lead of the jack seems to imply possession of the ten while denying the ace. East's refusal to play the ace does not deny his having it, and your best play is to finesse the nine of spades on the second round of the suit, hoping West has led from the jack-ten sequence.

Here again you played differently as a result of information gained—once from the auction and once from the opening lead.

You are again in four hearts. (partner forgot to leave you in three notrump).

NORTH
♠ K 7 4 2
♡ A Q 4
◇ K 3 2
♣ A 3 2

SOUTH
♠ 6 3
♡ K J 10 6 5
◇ A 6 5
♣ K 6 4

How do you play if:

(1) No opposing bidding. West leads the club queen.
(2) No opposing bidding. West leads the spade queen.
(3) East opens one club. West leads the club ten.

Answers:

(1) Unless you get some strong feeling (like someone shows you his hand), you should lead a spade to the king. This wins if West has the spade ace.

(2) The opening lead indicates that East has the spade ace, so nothing can be gained by covering. But if East has only two or three spades, you can get a spade trick by playing low twice and if necessary, trumping a third round in your hand. Hopefully the ace will drop. Now the spade king can be used to discard the club or diamond loser.

(3) This time the opening bid has told you where the ace of spades is. Unless East has psyched an opening bid he has that card, and playing to the spade king will be a foregone failure. It is correct to play as in example 2 and hope that the ace of spades falls on an early round.

Another game hand, this time four spades.

                    NORTH
                    ♠ A K 8
                    ♡ K 10 2
                    ◇ J 4 2
                    ♣ A 7 6 5

                    SOUTH
                    ♠ J 10 9 7 3
                    ♡ A Q 6
                    ◇ 9 5 3
                    ♣ K 10

How do you proceed in the given circumstances?

(1) No opposing bidding. West leads the club queen.
(2) No East-West bidding. West leads the spade six.
(3) East opened one club. West leads the club queen.

Answers:

(1) With no particular clues you should play the ace of spades to see if the queen drops. If it does not, finesse in spades and hope West has the spade queen with a maximum of three spades in his hand.
(2) West's lead of a spade would be very unusual if he has the queen. Here it would be right to play the ace and king of trumps and hope East has the queen either singleton or doubleton.

(3) East-West have only 15 points in high cards. West has led the club queen, meaning East has a maximum of 13. If West has the spade queen, then East has opened on a hand containing no more than 11 points. Unless East is a notoriously light opening bidder you should play the ace and king of trumps, hoping to drop the queen.

In this last hand you are in three notrump.

NORTH
♠ A 3 2
♡ 5 4 3
◊ K J 7 4
♣ 6 4 3

SOUTH
♠ K Q 8 5
♡ A Q 6
◊ A Q 10 3
♣ J 9

What considerations do you give to the following set of situations?

(1) No East-West bidding. West leads a diamond.
(2) No opposing bidding. West leads the spade nine.

Answers:

(1) With no information it is reasonable to play three rounds of spades. If they break, you have nine tricks and can decide if you wish to risk the heart finesse for an overtrick. If the spades do not divide, then you would take the heart finesse as the only way to make the contract. You might go down an extra trick or

two, but the finesse would be your best chance for the contract.

(2) Against the lead of the spade nine you could play exactly as you did above. This interesting lead, however, gives you an extra option that looks very good. It appears from the lead that East has the spade jack and ten. If you believe this to be true, you can win the opening lead with the ace in dummy and lead another spade with the intention of playing the eight unless East plays an honor. If East does play the jack or ten, you would enter dummy with a diamond to lead the last spade, again planning to play the eight if the remaining honor does not appear.

Throughout these hands your choice of plays was predicated on what you knew about the opponents' hands. Your information ranged from nothing at all, in which case you played normally, to an almost total concept of what was happening, in which case you could play a hand as if the opponents' cards were face up on the table, i.e., double-dummy. Your information became available from bids and plays that were made, and occasionally from bids and plays that were not made.

Some of the later chapters will demonstrate how to increase your initial overall knowledge of a hand and how to make the best use of what you know when further information is unavailable.

2

Finding the Witnesses

♠ ♡ ◇ ♣

When your dummy comes down you should always take a few seconds to consider how best to proceed. Tradition has it that certain habits must be adhered to. These habits include:

(1) Don't play too fast at trick one.
(2) Analyze the opening lead.
(3) Count your winners.
(4) Count your losers.
(5) Review the auction.

But doing all of these things will not help unless you pursue them to some conclusions. Not playing too fast is perhaps the most important, because it gives you time to engage the other habits. But just knowing that you have eight winners in a three notrump contract and that West probably has four hearts because he led the deuce will not help you win an extra trick. Having counted, analyzed, counted some more, and reviewed, you should then be involved in some thought processes like:

"I wonder why East didn't lead the spade king. He does not have both the ace and king."

"That's odd. East passed his partner's opening bid of one club and then led the ace of clubs. East cannot have any other high cards."

"Why didn't they bid spades? They have 22 high-card points and 10 spades. I guess the points must be divided evenly, and nobody has any distribution."

Thinking along lines such as these can frequently produce some rather astonishing results. On occasion you can tell where every missing ace, king, and queen is located before you have played from the dummy at trick one.

9

When you are playing in a suit contract, here are some general rules along these lines:

(1) The player who makes a nondescript opening lead does not have some holding such as A-K, K-Q, or Q-J of the suit led.

(2) The opening leader does not have the ace of the suit led when he leads a small card.

(3) If the opening leader does not lead an unbid suit, but instead leads a small card in some other suit, he does not have the ace and king or king and queen of an unbid suit.

If there has been some bidding by the opponent, you can consider that:

(1) An overcaller usually has a five-card or longer suit.

(2) A takeout doubler is likely to be short in the suit doubled.

(3) An opening bidder usually has 12 or more high-card points.

(4) A preempter generally has less than 10 high-card points.

(5) Someone who has bid notrump probably has a balanced hand with a specific range of high-card points.

As simple as these rules may sound, they must be recognized and considered when you are playing a dummy. Bear in mind that many auctions have fairly well described the strength of each of the opposing hands. For example:

(1) One-notrump opening bid: 15-18 high-card points or 12-14 or 16-18, etc.—the opponents must tell you the range they are using.

(2) One-notrump response to a suit: 6-10.

(3) A raise of partner's suit: 6-10.

(4) A pass of partner's opening bid: 0-5.

Let's take a look at a number of hands and see what can be

done by applying the above "rules." For the time being, our hand analysis will not go farther than trick one.

NORTH
♠ K 8 7 4
♡ 8 3
◊ J 7 2
♣ Q 10 8 3

SOUTH
♠ A Q J 10 3
♡ A 5 4
◊ Q 8
♣ K 5 4

SOUTH	WEST	NORTH	EAST
1 ♠	2 ♡	2 ♠	3 ♡
3 ♠	Pass	Pass	Pass

Opening lead: Heart six

The first example is an exercise in card location. West leads the six of hearts. Your first thought is that West cannot have some heart suit headed by the king-queen or by the queen-jack. If he had either of these combinations, the opening lead would have been an honor. When East plays the heart king on the trick, it should be apparent that East also has the heart jack—for, as noted, if West had the queen-jack he would have led the queen.

Now look at the diamond suit. While it is not a certainty, it is very likely that West does not have both the ace and king of diamonds. Holding them, West would have been inclined to lead the king rather than lead from an obviously bad heart holding (the raise from his partner notwithstanding).

So with very little difficulty you have concluded that East has the king and jack of hearts and either the ace or the king of diamonds. With these reasonably certain facts at your disposal, you can further conclude that West must have the club ace to justify his overcall. All of this may or may not have any bearing on this particular hand, but the thought processes used here are very important and should become second nature.

The complete deal was:

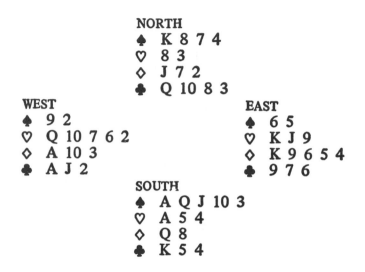

NORTH
♠ K 8 7 4
♡ 8 3
◇ J 7 2
♣ Q 10 8 3

WEST
♠ 9 2
♡ Q 10 7 6 2
◇ A 10 3
♣ A J 2

EAST
♠ 6 5
♡ K J 9
◇ K 9 6 5 4
♣ 9 7 6

SOUTH
♠ A Q J 10 3
♡ A 5 4
◇ Q 8
♣ K 5 4

It is very possible that you do not agree with the two-heart overcall with those West cards. However, it is not the worst bid ever made, and many players do bid on hands like this. Remember, though, that this book is concerned with working out what's happening at the table. It will have to take into consideration what people—your opponents—do or do not do. Players have styles and, regardless of whether they are right or wrong, they must not be ignored.

When an opponent has opened the bidding and has received a limited bid in response from his partner, you as declarer should form an opinion as to how much of the missing strength each defender is likely to hold. Here is an example:

NORTH
♠ K Q 4
♡ 10 8 6
◇ 8 7 6
♣ K Q J 4

SOUTH
♠ A 10 9 8 2
♡ 7 3
◇ K J
♣ A 10 8 3

WEST	NORTH	EAST	SOUTH
1 ♡	Pass	2 ♡	2 ♠
Pass	4 ♠	Pass	Pass
Pass			

Opening lead: Heart king

West leads the heart king, and when the dummy comes down, you make the observation that East-West have 17 high-card points between them. If West has an opening bid, then East has a rather minimum raise, which may or may not include the diamond ace or queen. West's continuation of hearts finds East with three—the queen, jack, and five. After trumping the third heart and drawing trumps (East had J-7-6 of spades), you are faced with a diamond guess. It is clear that to play East for the diamond ace is to play West for a 9-point opening bid. If East has the spade jack, the heart queen and jack, and the diamond ace, he has 8 of the missing 17 points.

The correct play therefore is to finesse the diamond jack. East is likely to have the diamond queen for his two-heart raise (and if West has both the ace and queen you can do nothing about it.)

The complete hand was:

```
                        NORTH
                        ♠  K Q 4
                        ♡  10 8 6
                        ◇  8 7 6
                        ♣  K Q J 4
        WEST                                EAST
        ♠  5 3                              ♠  J 7 6
        ♡  A K 9 4 2                        ♡  Q J 5
        ◇  A 10 9 3                         ◇  Q 5 4 2
        ♣  9 5                              ♣  7 6 2
                        SOUTH
                        ♠  A 10 9 8 2
                        ♡  7 3
                        ◇  K J
                        ♣  A 10 8 3
```

This habit of counting the opponents' total high cards and noting how many each opponent should have—and what each has in fact shown up with—is very important. It pays the biggest dividends when the opponents have bid and one of them has shown a limited hand. When that hands shows up with as much as it should hold, then you should play the partner for the rest of the cards. A player responds one notrump to his partner's diamond bid and shows up with an ace, a king, and a queen; that should be all he has. A player passes his partner's one-spade opening and shows up with an ace and a jack; he should not show up with any more.

NORTH
- ♠ A Q 10
- ♡ K J 10 4
- ◊ A 10 9
- ♣ K Q 4

SOUTH
- ♠ 9 8 6 5 4 3 2
- ♡ 8
- ◊ Q 8 6
- ♣ 8 5

WEST	NORTH	EAST	SOUTH
1 NT*	Double	2 ♣	2 ♠
Pass	4 ♠	Pass	Pass
Pass			

*15-17 points.

This hand brings into play the points made in the previous discussion.

Against your four spades, the opening lead of the club jack is covered in dummy and taken by East's ace. Your thoughts should be running along these lines: "East-West have 19 high-card points. West should have 15 to 17 of these for his opening one-notrump bid. As East has shown up with the club ace, this means West must have the remaining 15 points unless he's fooling around." When you gain the lead, you play a spade toward dummy; if West follows with the seven, you must play the ten on the assumption that West has all of the remaining high cards. If you did not bother to count the high cards and instead played the spade queen because "West should have the king for his one-notrump bid and whoever heard of a three-nothing break away," then you are being lazy in what should have been an easy hand.

When you are declarer, the easiest hands to play are those that begin with an opening notrump bid by an opponent. You should always be able to take advantage of the narrow range of high-card points promised.

The complete hand was:

```
                        NORTH
                        ♠ A Q 10
                        ♡ K J 10 4
                        ◇ A 10 9
                        ♣ K Q 4
       WEST                                EAST
       ♠ K J 7                             ♠ ——
       ♡ A Q 9 3                           ♡ 7 6 5 2
       ◇ K J 7                             ◇ 5 4 3 2
       ♣ J 10 9                            ♣ A 7 6 3 2
                        SOUTH
                        ♠ 9 8 6 5 4 3 2
                        ♡ 8
                        ◇ Q 8 6
                        ♣ 8 5
```

In this case West's lead happened to pinpoint East's ace of clubs. At trick one you know where every card in the deck was located. Unfortunately, most hands do not expose themselves as quickly and easily as this one. A later chapter will deal with the technique of looking further into the opponents' cards.

Having seen the basic ideas behind locating or placing cards in an opponent's hand, we can take a look at some cases from actual play.

NORTH
♠ 9 2
♡ 10 6 4 3
◊ J 8 2
♣ A Q J 3

SOUTH
♠ A 7
♡ A K Q 9 5 2
◊ Q 10 5 3
♣ 4

WEST	NORTH	EAST	SOUTH
Pass	Pass	Pass	1 ♡
1 ♠	2 ♡	4 ♠	5 ♡
Pass	Pass	Pass	

Opening lead: Spade six

Your unkind opponents have jammed the bidding, and you find yourself in an uncomfortable contract of five hearts. West's opening lead of the spade six goes to East's king and your ace. Trumps divide two-one with West having the doubleton jack. Your problem: Who has the king of clubs? If West has it, a simple finesse will work. If East has it, you will have to play the ace and lead the queen, intending to throw your spade loser if East does not cover with the king.

What do you do? And most important, why? Before going on to the next paragraph, make up your mind as to what you know about the East-West cards.

The things that you should be considering are:

(1) West's lead of the spade six has denied the

queen-jack combination, thus marking East with the spade jack as well as the king.

(2) West did not lead a diamond honor. He probably does not have both the ace and the king.

If West has a spade suit headed at best by the queen and only one high diamond, it is almost a certainty that he has the club king in addition. Otherwise he would not be close to having an overcall (remember that East is the opponent with the singleton heart as added distributional value). The correct play is to take the club finesse against West.

The complete hand was:

```
                    NORTH
                    ♠  9 2
                    ♡  10 6 4 3
                    ◇  J 8 2
                    ♣  A Q J 3
        WEST                          EAST
        ♠  Q 10 8 6 3                 ♠  K J 5 4
        ♡  J 7                        ♡  8
        ◇  A 9 4                      ◇  K 7 6
        ♣  K 7 6                      ♣  10 9 8 5 2
                    SOUTH
                    ♠  A 7
                    ♡  A K Q 9 5 2
                    ◇  Q 10 5 3
                    ♣  4
```

If you have doubts about the accuracy of these deductions, you can measure it by asking yourself these questions:

(1) What would I lead from?

```
        ♠  Q 10 8 6 3
        ♡  J 7
        ◇  A K 9
        ♣  7 6 2
```

If you would lead the diamond king, and will agree you probably do not have the ace and the king when you lead a spade, then you can ask:

> (2)   Would I bid one spade over one heart (or would I expect others to do so)?

Holding only:

♠ Q 10 8 6 3
♡ J 7
◇ A 9 4
♣ 7 6 2

NORTH
♠ K Q 5
♡ 6 2
◇ K 10 8 3
♣ Q 10 3 2

SOUTH
♠ A J 10 9 4
♡ 9 7
◇ J 7 5
♣ K 9 4

WEST	NORTH	EAST	SOUTH
1 ♡	Pass	2 ♡	2 ♠
Pass	3 ♠	Pass	Pass
Pass			

Opening lead: Heart four

Occasionally you may play a hand where every important card is known to you as early as trick one. This is one of those cases. West's lead is the heart four, and your first thought is that East must have the heart ace, since West would not underlead it. Why hasn't West led a heart honor? Because he does not have a sequence of honors. West does not have the heart ace-king, king-queen, or queen-jack. When East puts up the heart king as trick one, you know that he also has the ace and the jack. This accounts for 8 of the 21 outstanding high-card points, leaving the opening bidder with a maximum of 13. Considering these facts, you have to decide if you wish to try to throw a club loser on a diamond or whether you would rather throw a diamond loser on a club. It is barely possible that East has the club jack (which would leave West with only 12 points), but it is most unlikely that East has the diamond queen (which would leave West with 11 high-card points). Furthermore, if East did hold the diamond queen in addition to his heart honors, he would probably have bid more than two hearts. With this in mind, you should lead a low diamond toward the ten, hoping to find West with the ace-queen doubleton or ace-queen third. If West turns out to have four diamonds to the ace-queen, you will have to guess the clubs in order to make your contract.

There is one more point to be made here:

(1)   Do you know how many hearts East has? Which heart was led? West led the heart four. By the rule of eleven, you know there are seven hearts higher than the four-spot in the remaining three hands. You and dummy have only three of them, so East must have the other four. (It is possible, of course, that East has *five* hearts—until you ask yourself if West would open the bidding on a queen-high four-card suit.)

The complete hand was:

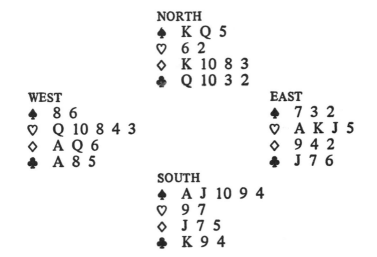

NORTH
♠ K Q 5
♡ 6 2
♢ K 10 8 3
♣ Q 10 3 2

WEST
♠ 8 6
♡ Q 10 8 4 3
♢ A Q 6
♣ A 8 5

EAST
♠ 7 3 2
♡ A K J 5
♢ 9 4 2
♣ J 7 6

SOUTH
♠ A J 10 9 4
♡ 9 7
♢ J 7 5
♣ K 9 4

Here is another hand that quickly surrenders all its secrets to a discerning declarer.

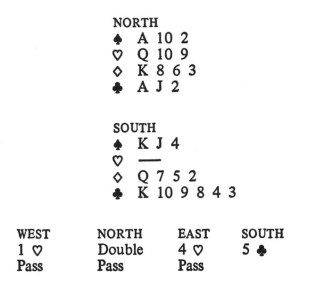

NORTH
♠ A 10 2
♡ Q 10 9
♦ K 8 6 3
♣ A J 2

SOUTH
♠ K J 4
♡ —
♦ Q 7 5 2
♣ K 10 9 8 4 3

WEST	NORTH	EAST	SOUTH
1 ♡	Double	4 ♡	5 ♣
Pass	Pass	Pass	

Opening lead: Heart five

After this somewhat spirited auction, West starts off with the heart five. The heart ten from dummy gets the jack from East. A count of high-card points finds East-West with 17. What do you know for sure about the opponents' hands? Who has the heart ace? West does not have the ace and king of hearts, as he would not underlead them; nor can he have the ace of hearts (for the same reason). So East is marked with the ace and jack of hearts, which gives West a maximum of 12 high-card points. It would be very difficult to find an opening bid that did not include both black queens, and you should finesse West for both of them.

The complete hand was:

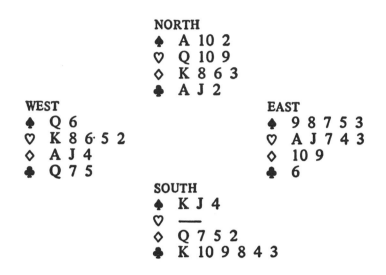

NORTH
♠ A 10 2
♡ Q 10 9
♢ K 8 6 3
♣ A J 2

WEST
♠ Q 6
♡ K 8 6 5 2
♢ A J 4
♣ Q 7 5

EAST
♠ 9 8 7 5 3
♡ A J 7 4 3
♢ 10 9
♣ 6

SOUTH
♠ K J 4
♡ —
♢ Q 7 5 2
♣ K 10 9 8 4 3

East might play the heart ace at trick one. This could cause South to credit West with the jack, and might confuse the issue enough to lead declarer astray. It is unlikely, but a chance nonetheless.

So far the clues considered have been along the lines of opening leads that were made, or leads that were not made.

Very frequently a hand comes along on which you obtain some information because of a *bid* that was or *was not* made. (Later in the book there will be an in-depth look at this aspect. Some hands in this area, however, are suitable for consideration now.)

NORTH
- ♠ Q 9 7
- ♡ A J 4 2
- ◇ 7 6 2
- ♣ Q 8 3

SOUTH
- ♠ J 8 3
- ♡ Q 10 9 7 5
- ◇ A K 4
- ♣ A K

SOUTH	WEST	NORTH	EAST
1 ♡	Pass	2 ♡	Pass
4 ♡	Pass	Pass	Pass

Opening lead: Spade king

Against four hearts, West starts with the king and ace of spades, East following with the ten and five, and continues with a third spade ruffed by East with the heart six. The diamond ten return is taken by your ace, and you lead the heart queen, West following peacefully with the three. Before playing from dummy, you should consider what has happened and decide if you have any reason not to take the normal finesse.

West, who did not bid over one heart, has shown up with five spades to the ace-king. East's return of the diamond ten would seem to indicate that West has either the jack (if East is leading from Q-10-9) or the queen-jack (if East is leading from 10-9-8). If West also has the king of hearts, along with his proven values, he might very well have overcalled with one spade. On these reasonable premises, you should play the heart ace and hope that East's original holding was king-six doubleton. If West turns out to have started with the heart king, you should congratulate him on a well-judged pass of one heart. A player who passes when holding the West cards plus the heart king should be encouraged to do so. The last thing anyone should want is to have opponents overcalling and trying to clutter up the otherwise smooth and unimpeded auctions we would all rather have. The occasional loss (as on this hand if West holds the heart king) will be more than repaid by the numerous part-scores your side is allowed to play, to say nothing of a large number of good games and saves missed by your conservative friend.

The complete hand was:

```
                      NORTH
                      ♠ Q 9 7
                      ♡ A J 4 2
                      ◇ 7 6 2
                      ♣ Q 8 3
WEST                                    EAST
♠ A K 6 4 2                             ♠ 10 5
♡ 8 3                                   ♡ K 6
◇ J 5 3                                 ◇ Q 10 9 8
♣ 10 4 2                                ♣ J 9 7 6 5
                      SOUTH
                      ♠ J 8 3
                      ♡ Q 10 9 7 5
                      ◇ A K 4
                      ♣ A K
```

Again you must ask yourself, "Would I bid one spade over a heart with:

```
♠ A K 6 4 2
♡ K 3
◇ J 5 3
♣ 10 4 2
```

and how many other people would bid?"

The hand that passes up an opportunity to bid is often at least as enlightening as a hand that has bid—and sometimes more so. Here is another example that comes up with reasonable frequency.

NORTH
♠ A 5 3
♡ A 9 6 2
◇ J 6 4 3
♣ Q 6

SOUTH
♠ J 8 2
♡ K J 10 5 3
◇ A K 10
♣ 10 2

WEST	NORTH	EAST	SOUTH
1 ♠	Pass	Pass	2 ♡
Pass	3 ♡	Pass	4 ♡
Pass	Pass	Pass	

Opening lead: Spade six

Against four hearts, West leads the spade six. From the lead you can conclude that West does not have both the king and queen of spades. What else do you know? West apparently has made a lead from just one spade honor. Surely if he had had a better lead he would have selected something else. With the ace and king of clubs, a club lead would have been much more appealing than the spade. So you are now playing on the near certainty that East has a spade honor and a club honor. You can even tell which honors East holds. As East could not respond to his partner's bid of one spade, he cannot have more than 5 points, and the only way he can have just 5 points is if he has the spade queen and club king.

Knowing that East has these cards dictates that you play West for the rest. You must not take the diamond finesse, but instead play off the ace and king in the hope that West began with the singleton or doubleton queen (as the jack will provide a parking place for a black-suit loser). Likewise, in hearts you play the king and lead the jack. If the queen does not come up—take a finesse.

The complete hand was:

```
                    NORTH
                    ♠ A 5 3
                    ♡ A 9 6 2
                    ◇ J 6 4 3
                    ♣ Q 6
        WEST                        EAST
        ♠ K 10 7 6 4                ♠ Q 9
        ♡ Q 8                       ♡ 7 4
        ◇ Q 7                       ◇ 9 8 5 2
        ♣ A J 5 4                   ♣ K 9 8 7 3
                    SOUTH
                    ♠ J 8 2
                    ♡ K J 10 5 3
                    ◇ A K 10
                    ♣ 10 2
```

Note how different this hand would have been to play had West led the king and ace of clubs, then shifted to the king of spades. You would then be faced with a situation in which you had practically no clues. East could very well hold the red queens and the club jack. Or East could hold any combination of them. Or he could have none of them.

NORTH
♠ Q 5
♡ Q 9 7 6
◇ A 10
♣ 9 5 4 3 2

SOUTH
♠ A 7
♡ A J 10 8 5 4
◇ K J 3
♣ 10 8

WEST	NORTH	EAST	SOUTH
1 ♠	Pass	2 ♠	3 ♡
Pass	4 ♡	Pass	Pass
Pass			

Opening lead: Spade six

This last hand is one of the finest examples I have ever seen of placing cards early in a hand. My teammate, Billy Eisenberg, played this hand in an important match against good opposition. He drew the correct inferences and played accordingly. Before you read on, why not study this hand and determine your line of play? Just apply the principles from this chapter on locating cards and proceed. The opening lead is the spade six and East covers dummy's queen with the king. Ready to play?

OK! Eisenberg's thoughts went: "I'm missing 19 high-card points; and from the play to trick one, East is known to have 3 points in spades. Since West did not lead a club, I cannot expect him to hold both the ace and king; so I can place East with *at least* another three points in clubs. East cannot hold the heart king, as that would give him a minimum of 9 high-card points and it also would give West a 10-point opening bid, which would be most unreasonable. So there is no reason to take the heart finesse. If I lay down the ace of hearts and the king does not fall, I can always play the ace of diamonds and finesse the jack on the way back. I'm really inclined, however, to play West for the queen of diamonds. The problem is, in order to finesse West for the queen of diamonds I can't lay down the ace of hearts because that is the only entry back to my hand."

So Eisenberg won the spade ace, and at trick two he finessed the diamond ten. This would win unless West had started with only 11 points in high cards. In fact, it did win; and after South cashed the diamond ace, the heart ace was the entry to his hand to use the diamond king for a spade discard. As can be seen from the diagram, you cannot afford to play in any other sequence.

The complete hand was:

```
                         NORTH
                         ♠ Q 5
                         ♡ Q 9 7 6
                         ◊ A 10
                         ♣ 9 5 4 3 2
         WEST                              EAST
         ♠ J 9 8 6 2                       ♠ K 10 4 3
         ♡ K 3                             ♡ 2
         ◊ Q 8 5                           ◊ 9 7 6 4 2
         ♣ A Q J                           ♣ K 7 6
                         SOUTH
                         ♠ A 7
                         ♡ A J 10 8 5 4
                         ◊ K J 3
                         ♣ 10 8
```

Once Billy drew the reasonable inferences from the spade lead and the non-club lead, it was not difficult to pursue the logic to a successful conclusion.

♠ ♡ ◇ ♣

The following quiz and the ensuing quizzes will all be concerned with the chapter at hand. Each quiz will have a format. The hands are presented with appropriate information, and questions are asked which you should answer before proceeding. In some of the quizzes there will be hands that consist of facts only. You will be expected to indicate how you intend to approach the hand. Make up your own questions. Answer the questions. Then go to the next page for the correct questions. These are the only quizzes in the world that have questions for answers. If your questions are correct, look next to see if your answers are also correct. As each chapter from here on will depend somewhat on previous chapters, you would do well not to proceed until you are sure you understand the material. Don't worry if you make some errors in the quiz. All that is necessary is that you understand the explanations. Later, when you play, you will discover that the concepts will begin to fall nicely into place. All set?

♠ ♡ ◇ ♣

Quiz

NORTH
♠ A J 8 4
♡ A K 3
♢ Q 10 9 5
♣ Q 4

SOUTH
♠ Q 10 9 7 3
♡ Q 4
♢ K 4
♣ 7 6 3 2

EAST	SOUTH	WEST	NORTH
1 ♣	Pass	Pass	Double
Pass	1 ♠	Pass	3 ♠
Pass	4 ♠	Pass	Pass
Pass			

West leads the club ace. East plays the eight. West continues the club nine to East's king. East exits with the heart jack.

1. How did the bidding go?

2. How many high cards do you have? How many do they have?

3. What is the most high-card points that West is likely to have?

4. Which suit will determine your success?

5. What was the opening lead?

6. Who has the spade king?

7. Who has the diamond ace?

8. How do you play?

Answers

```
                    NORTH
                    ♠ A J 8 4
                    ♡ A K 3
                    ◇ Q 10 9 5
                    ♣ Q 4
WEST                                    EAST
♠ 6 5 2                                 ♠ K
♡ 8 6 5 2                               ♡ J 10 9 7
◇ 8 7 3 2                               ◇ A J 6
♣ A 9                                   ♣ K J 10 8 5
                    SOUTH
                    ♠ Q 10 9 7 3
                    ♡ Q 4
                    ◇ K 4
                    ♣ 7 6 3 2
```

1. Did you or did you not remember the auction?
2. You have 23 high-card points. They have 17.
3. West should not have more than 5 high-card points because he passed one club.
4. The spade suit is the key suit.
5. The club ace was the opening lead.
6. East—the club ace and the spade king would give West a bid in response to one club, and would mean East had opened the bidding on 10 high-card points.
7. East—same reasoning as above.
8. Try to drop the singleton king of spades in East's hand.

Quiz

NORTH
♠ A Q 4 2
♡ 8 7
◇ K J 8 6
♣ Q 10 4

SOUTH
♠ K J 10 7 3
♡ 10
◇ 10 4
♣ K J 9 8 3

Neither side vulnerable

NORTH	EAST	SOUTH	WEST
1 ◇	Pass	1 ♠	Pass
2 ♠	Pass	4 ♠	Pass
Pass	Pass		

Neither side vulnerable against your aggressive four-spade contract, West leads the heart two.

1. Who has the heart ace?

2. What heart honors does East have?

3. How many hearts does East have?

4. Who has the club ace?

5. Who has the diamond ace?
   East takes the first trick with the heart ace.

6. Who has the heart queen?

7. How will you play this contract?

Answers

```
                      NORTH
                      ♠ A Q 4 2
                      ♡ 8 7
                      ◊ K J 8 6
                      ♣ Q 10 4
WEST                                      EAST
♠ 8 5                                     ♠ 9 6
♡ K J 9 2                                 ♡ A Q 6 5 4 3
◊ A 7 3 2                                 ◊ Q 9 5
♣ A 7 2                                   ♣ 6 5
                      SOUTH
                      ♠ K J 10 7 3
                      ♡ 10
                      ◊ 10 4
                      ♣ K J 9 8 3
```

1. East has the heart ace. West would not underlead it.
2. West would not lead low from the K-Q of hearts or the Q-J of hearts. West is leading from K-x-x-x, Q-x-x-x, or K-J-x-x. This means East has A-K-J, A-Q-J, or A-Q.
3. West's lead of the heart two shows he has four of that suit, leaving East with six.
4. West has the club ace. East would overcall the one-diamond opening bid if he held six good hearts and the club ace.
5. West has the diamond ace. Same reasoning.
6. East has the heart queen. East's play of the ace implies West has the king. West would lead the king if holding the K-Q, which means the queen is with East.
7. Draw trumps as soon as possible and play West for the diamond ace.

Quiz

NORTH
♠ Q 7 6 4 3
♡ K 5
◇ 9 6 2
♣ Q 6 5

SOUTH
♠ 9
♡ A J 10 9 6 4
◇ A K 3
♣ 9 4 2

WEST	NORTH	EAST	SOUTH
1 ♠	Pass	1NT	2 ♡
Pass	Pass	Pass	

Opening lead: Diamond jack

1. Who has the diamond queen?

2. Who has the spade ace?

3. Who has the spade king?

4. Who has the club ace?

5. Who has the club king?

6. Who has the heart queen?

7. How do you play?

Answers

```
                        NORTH
                        ♠ Q 7 6 4 3
                        ♡ K 5
                        ◇ 9 6 2
                        ♣ Q 6 5
WEST                                        EAST
♠ A J 10 8 2                                ♠ K 5
♡ Q 8 7                                     ♡ 3 2
◇ J 10 8                                    ◇ Q 7 5 4
♣ A J                                       ♣ K 10 8 7 3
                        SOUTH
                        ♠ 9
                        ♡ A J 10 9 6 4
                        ◇ A K 3
                        ♣ 9 4 2
```

1. East has the diamond queen. West's lead of the jack denies it.

2 & 3. It is not exactly clear what is happening in the spade suit. But this much you can tell: West does not have the ace and king of spades, or else he would have led one. Therefore East has one or both of them.

4 & 5. For the same reasons as above, East has one or both of the club honors. You know East has the diamond queen and at least one honor in both clubs and spades. For two reasons it looks like West must have an honor in clubs and spades as well: West opened the bidding and cannot have an opening bid without cards in clubs *and* spades (since he hasn't both the ace and king in either suit). Also, East would have bid more than one notrump if he held any more high cards than in fact he does have.

6. West has the heart queen. You are missing 21 high-card points. East has the diamond queen and

at least the king of spades (maybe the ace) and *at least* the king of clubs (maybe the ace), which means he has at least 8 points. If he had the heart queen also he would have 10 points, leaving West with 11 for his opening bid.

7.   Lead the heart jack from your hand and take a finesse. If West has three hearts this will be necessary.

Quiz

NORTH
♠ J 7 6 4
♡ A K 10
◇ Q 10 4
♣ 7 6 5

SOUTH
♠ 10
♡ J 9 8 7 6 5
◇ K 8 5
♣ A K J

WEST	NORTH	EAST	SOUTH
1 ♠	Pass	2 ♠	3 ♡
Pass	4 ♡	Pass	Pass
Pass			

Opening lead: Spade five

West leads the spade five and East plays the ace. East returns the club ten.

Decide what questions you need answered in order to come up with the best line of play. Then answer the questions. It may help if you write them down.

```
                         NORTH
                         ♠ J 7 6 4
                         ♡ A K 10
                         ◊ Q 10 4
                         ♣ 7 6 5
      WEST                                    EAST
      ♠ K 9 8 5 2                             ♠ A Q 3
      ♡ Q 4 2                                 ♡ 3
      ◊ A J 3                                 ◊ 9 7 6 2
      ♣ Q 4                                   ♣ 10 9 8 3 2
                         SOUTH
                         ♠ 10
                         ♡ J 9 8 7 6 5
                         ◊ K 8 5
                         ♣ A K J
```

East wins the first trick with the ace of spades and returns the club ten.

Questions and Answers:

> 1. What's happening in spades?
>   1. East must have the spade queen also. West would not lead low from the king and queen.
> 2. What high cards am I missing?
>   2. Eighteen, of which East has already shown at least 6.
> 3. Who has the club queen?
> 4. Who has the heart queen?
> 5. Who has the diamond ace?
>   3, 4, 5. West must have all of these cards because the absence of any one of them would mean the opening bid was made on a 10-point hand at best.
> 6. How about the diamond jack?
>   6. West probably has it.
> 7. What line do you take?
>   7. Finesse in hearts against West's queen. But try to drop the queen of clubs. Don't finesse here—East cannot have the black lady. After

you have done all of this, you can decide whether to play West for the diamond jack, in which case you take a finesse. Or you can play West for a doubleton diamond. Then lead up to the queen and duck on the way back, hoping the ace will drop.

Quiz

NORTH
♠ 7 6
♡ 8 2
◊ Q 10 9 4
♣ A K J 10 7

SOUTH
♠ A 5 4
♡ Q 7 3
◊ A K J 8 3
♣ 6 2

Neither side vulnerable

WEST	NORTH	EAST	SOUTH
Pass	Pass	Pass	1 ◊
Double	Redouble	2 ♡	Pass
Pass	3 ◊	3 ♡	4 ◊
Pass	5 ◊	Pass	Pass
Pass			

Opening lead: Spade queen

As for the previous hand, you should try to come up with a series of questions which, if answered properly, will indicate the correct line.

Without peeking ahead, write down at least the gist of what you are thinking. This makes you work just that little bit harder—and makes so much difference.

NORTH
- ♠ 7 6
- ♡ 8 2
- ◊ Q 10 9 4
- ♣ A K J 10 7

WEST
- ♠ Q J 10 3
- ♡ A J 4
- ◊ 7
- ♣ Q 9 8 5 4

EAST
- ♠ K 9 8 2
- ♡ K 10 9 6 5
- ◊ 6 5 2
- ♣ 3

SOUTH
- ♠ A 5 4
- ♡ Q 7 3
- ◊ A K J 8 3
- ♣ 6 2

Fortunately, this is not a book on bidding—that is the way it went. Even if you do not approve of some of the actions taken, the information has been made available and your questions and answers should look something like these.

Questions and Answers:

1. What's happening in spades?
   1. West has the queen-jack, and East has the king.
2. What's happening in hearts?
   2. West would lead a heart honor if he held both the ace and the king, so East has at least one of them.
3. Can East have both the ace and the king of hearts?
   3. No. West made a takeout double and cannot have enough for his bid without one heart honor.
4. Who has the queen of clubs?
   4. West will have it almost all of the time. In the actual hand the club queen gives him only 10 high-card points. Notice also that the jack of hearts might be with East, giving West only 9 points.

5. How will you play this hand?
    5. You are going to need four club tricks. Normally you might play the ace and king before leading the jack, reserving your decision and hoping to ruff out the queen if it does not drop. Here, however, you can be sure West will have long clubs, and the normal play will not work. So you will have to take a finesse in clubs.

6. Should you take a safety play in clubs by first laying down the ace?
    6. No. There is too great a chance that West will have five clubs.

7. What then is the correct line?
    7. Win the spade lead. Play two trumps, ending in your hand. When they do not break, you must finesse the ten of clubs now and come back to your hand with a trump (drawing the last trump in the process). Now another club finesse allows you to discard two spades (or hearts) and there is still a trump in dummy to take care of the last loser.

3

Analyzing the Clues

♠ ♡ ◇ ♣

You have studied the dummy and the opening lead and you have drawn a rough picture of what you think is going on and what you need to do. The play at trick one is concluded and, depending on what happened, you may have made some small adjustment in your overall view of the hand. You are now ready to proceed. But before you play on, take this little quiz on opening leads.

This quiz is divided into two parts, both rather similar. Do not give too much thought to your answers as there is not always a right or wrong lead and there are no catches whatsoever to worry about.

The auction in the following hands has been the same. Your partner opens one heart and RHO (right-hand opponent) overcalls one spade; you raise to two hearts and your LHO (left-hand opponent) bids two spades, which is passed out.

PARTNER	RHO	YOU	LHO
1 ♡	1 ♠	2 ♡	2 ♠
Pass	Pass	Pass	

What lead do you make with the following hands:

(1) ♠ J 7 6
♡ Q 9 7 2
◇ K 8 6
♣ 5 4 3

(2) ♠ 8 7
♡ 10 9 8 7
◇ Q 10 8 6
♣ K 3 2

(3) ♠ 7 4 2
♡ A 9 7
◇ J 10 9 8
♣ Q 7 6

(4) ♠ K 4 2   (5) ♠ 10 4   (6) ♠ 10 8 2
    ♡ 9 6 4 2   ♡ 10 8 7 6 3   ♡ A J 4 3
    ◇ J 9 7 5 3   ◇ Q J 10   ◇ 8 6
    ♣ 8   ♣ Q 9 7   ♣ J 9 7 6

(7) ♠ 4 2   (8) ♠ J 8 2   (9) ♠ 8 6 3
    ♡ K 9 7   ♡ J 8 3   ♡ A Q 3
    ◇ Q J 7 4   ◇ K Q J 7   ◇ 10 8 4 2
    ♣ 10 8 7 6   ♣ 9 4 2   ♣ 10 9 8

Answers:

(1) ♡ 2   (2) ♡ 10   (3) ◇ J
(4) ♣ 8   (5) ◇ Q   (6) ◇ 8
(7) ♡ 7   (8) ◇ K   (9) ♣ 10

This time the auction is slightly different. One heart by you, pass, two hearts by your partner, two spades by your RHO, all pass.

YOU	LHO	PARTNER	RHO
1 ♡	Pass	2 ♡	2 ♠
Pass	Pass	Pass	

It is your opening lead holding the following hands:

(1) ♠ 8 4   (2) ♠ A 10 4   (3) ♠ K J 2
    ♡ A Q 8 6 2   ♡ K J 8 6 3   ♡ K Q 8 4 3
    ◇ K Q 10   ◇ K J 9   ◇ 5 3
    ♣ J 8 6   ♣ 4 2   ♣ K 10 2

(4) ♠ A 8 3   (5) ♠ A 4 2   (6) ♠ A K 2
    ♡ K Q 4 3 2   ♡ A 10 8 7 3   ♡ J 8 7 4 3
    ◇ 4   ◇ 9 2   ◇ 9 3
    ♣ Q 8 6 3   ♣ K J 7   ♣ K J 7

(7) ♠ J 3   (8) ♠ 9 8 3   (9) ♠ A 3
    ♡ K Q 10 4 3   ♡ A Q 8 6 2   ♡ Q 8 7 6 4
    ◇ 5 4 2   ◇ 4 3   ◇ Q J 10 9
    ♣ A K J   ♣ A K 5   ♣ A 8

Answers:

(1) ◇ K   (2) ♡ 6   (3) ♡ K
(4) ◇ 4   (5) ◇ 9   (6) ◇ 9
(7) ♣ K   (8) ♣ K   (9) ◇ Q

The point of this quiz is an important one. It is the answer to the question you should ask yourself when your opponents, who have bid and raised hearts, lead something else. "Why didn't I get a heart lead?" Well? On the hands you just examined, what caused you to lead something other than the suit your side bid?

There were a number of reasons for another lead, and, as declarer, you should know what they might be.

(1) The opening leader had an alternate lead that seemed more constructive. You can always identify this because the lead is obviously from some honor combination such as K-Q-J, A-K-10, Q-J-10-9, or on occasion, J-10-9-x.

(2) The opening leader had a singleton or perhaps a doubleton. Again, you can usually tell a short-suit lead because your side rates to have quite a few cards in this suit.

(3) The opening leader had the ace of the suit (without the king) and decided not to lead it. This is a frequent case, and the clue to it is identifying what turns out to be a neutral opening lead. West may lead a trump, or he may lead from some nebulous holding in an unbid suit. For some reason he did not want to lead his (their) suit.

The above rules apply more strongly when you have the weaker of your opponents' hands on lead. A hand that raised one heart to two hearts will seldom have a good lead other than hearts, and his lead of another suit will more often than not be a singleton or an unwillingness to lead the ace of hearts. The hand that opened the bidding, however, is frequently going to have a good alternate lead. Even so, if the opening bidder makes a neutral lead, or an aggressive lead, and then does not shift to hearts when it appears he should, you can almost for a certainty play him for the ace.

NORTH
♠ K 10 8
♡ K 7 4
♢ 7 3
♣ K J 10 7 3

SOUTH
♠ A 9 7 6 5 3
♡ J 2
♢ A 8 6
♣ Q 2

WEST	NORTH	EAST	SOUTH
1 ♡	Pass	2 ♡	2 ♠
Pass	4 ♠	Pass	Pass
Pass			

West leads the diamond four and East plays the king. West has led a diamond from a holding of Q-J-x-x or Q-10-x-x, with the second holding being more likely since West might have led the queen had he held queen-jack. Regardless of what else you may learn about the hand, you may play with the almost certain knowledge that the heart ace is with West. "Why can't East have it?" you may ask. Because West would be much more inclined to lead a heart from Q-x-x-x-x or Q-10-x-x-x, a suit which has been raised, than a diamond from Q-10-x-x, which could turn out to be the opponents' main side suit. Incidentally, you should be aware that West must have at least one of the two missing heart honors because the lack of both would mean he had opened the bidding on 10 high-card points.

The entire hand was:

```
                    NORTH
                    ♠ K 10 8
                    ♡ K 7 4
                    ◇ 7 3
                    ♣ K J 10 7 3
    WEST                              EAST
    ♠ Q 4                            ♠ J 2
    ♡ A 10 9 8 3                     ♡ Q 6 5
    ◇ Q 10 5 4                       ◇ K J 9 2
    ♣ A 9                            ♣ 8 6 5 4
                    SOUTH
                    ♠ A 9 7 6 5 3
                    ♡ J 2
                    ◇ A 8 6
                    ♣ Q 2
```

NORTH
- ♠ K 7 5 4
- ♡ 8 3
- ◊ A 8 7
- ♣ Q 6 4 2

SOUTH
- ♠ A Q 9 6 2
- ♡ K J 4
- ◊ 5 3
- ♣ 9 5 3

EAST	SOUTH	WEST	NORTH
1 ♡	1 ♠	2 ♡	2 ♠
Pass	Pass	Pass	

Opening lead: Diamond jack

After you have won the diamond ace and drawn trumps, which divide two-two, the jack in East's hand, you will exit with a diamond. East will win and probably lead a heart. You would like to have had more time to make a decision about the missing high hearts, but you didn't get it. So what do you know about this hand?

(1) East has the king and queen of diamonds.
(2) East has the ace or king of clubs—maybe both—as West did not lead one.
(3) The diamond cannot be a singleton or a doubleton.

So it appears that West has either both heart honors, or one of them plus one club honor. If you work on the above theory, you will play West for the heart ace.

The whole hand was:

NORTH
♠ K 7 5 4
♡ 8 3
◊ A 8 7
♣ Q 6 4 2

WEST
♠ 10 8
♡ A 9 2
◊ J 10 9 6 2
♣ K 10 8

EAST
♠ J 3
♡ Q 10 7 6 5
◊ K Q 4
♣ A J 7

SOUTH
♠ A Q 9 6 2
♡ K J 4
◊ 5 3
♣ 9 5 3

NORTH
♠ 8 6 4 2
♡ A 3
◊ A Q J 10 5 4
♣ 8

SOUTH
♠ A K J 3
♡ J 7
◊ 8 2
♣ Q J 5 4 3

NORTH	EAST	SOUTH	WEST
1 ◊	1 ♡	2 ♣	2 ♡
Pass	Pass	2 ♠	3 ♡
3 ♠	Pass	4 ♠	Pass
Pass	Pass		

After a rather winding auction, West selects the diamond three as his opening lead. Ask yourself the standard question for this situation: "Why didn't West lead a heart?" The answer is not too difficult. This lead is clearly a singleton, and there could be no conceivable reason to lead from any other diamond combination that might include the king.

How would you expect trumps to break? Which opponent is more likely to have four and how will you play?

The one person who cannot have four trumps is East. This would leave West with a singleton spade as well as a singleton diamond, which would be inconsistent with a mere raise to two hearts. Furthermore, a four-card spade suit in West's hand is very unlikely, as defenders do not usually try for ruffs when holding good trumps. So with trumps apparently three-two you can guarantee your contract by refusing the diamond finesse and then playing the ace and king of trumps, refusing this finesse also. When the queen of spades does not drop, you just concede a diamond to East. Later, your heart loser goes on the diamond suit while West ruffs in. After losing a club, your dummy will be good.

The entire hand was about as you expected:

```
                        NORTH
                        ♠ 8 6 4 2
                        ♡ A 3
                        ◊ A Q J 10 5 4
                        ♣ 8
WEST                                          EAST
♠ Q 10 5                                      ♠ 9 7
♡ 10 9 6 2                                    ♡ K Q 8 5 4
◊ 3                                           ◊ K 9 7 6
♣ K 10 7 6 2                                  ♣ A 9
                        SOUTH
                        ♠ A K J 3
                        ♡ J 7
                        ◊ 8 2
                        ♣ Q J 5 4 3
```

As can be seen from the four hands, you will go down if you take either the diamond or the spade finesse. A diamond finesse lets East give West a diamond ruff; then a club to the ace lets East lead another diamond, and now West must make his spade queen. If you took the diamond ace at trick one and played a spade to the jack, West would win and then put East in with a club. He would cash the diamond king and lead another diamond with the same result as before—the ten of spades would be promoted.

West chose a very poor moment for his lead. West was likely to win a trump trick anyway, and his lead gave you time to dispose of the heart loser.

```
                    NORTH
                    ♠  J 10 2
                    ♡  Q 10 8
                    ◇  K Q
                    ♣  9 6 4 3 2


                    SOUTH
                    ♠  K 3
                    ♡  K J 7 6 5 3
                    ◇  10 4 3
                    ♣  A 8
```

EAST	SOUTH	WEST	NORTH
1 ♠	2 ♡	2 ♠	3 ♡
Pass	Pass	Pass	

West leads the diamond nine to East's ace. East returns the spade six, and it is your guess. A quick look at the circumstances should give you the answer. It is clear that West's lead is not "constructive," *i.e.*, from some combination of high cards; nor can it possibly be either a singleton or a doubleton. It is clearly a neutral, noncommittal lead.

This almost always indicates that West was worried about leading spades, his partner's suit. As you have seen, this tends to imply the ace. Your correct play is amost certainly the three of spades.

The entire hand was:

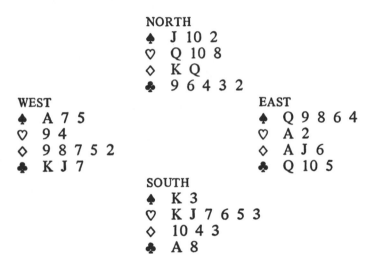

NORTH
♠ J 10 2
♡ Q 10 8
◇ K Q
♣ 9 6 4 3 2

WEST
♠ A 7 5
♡ 9 4
◇ 9 8 7 5 2
♣ K J 7

EAST
♠ Q 9 8 6 4
♡ A 2
◇ A J 6
♣ Q 10 5

SOUTH
♠ K 3
♡ K J 7 6 5 3
◇ 10 4 3
♣ A 8

Do not follow these rules blindly, however. Their usual good counsel may occasionally lead into a trap. Instead, regard them as strong suggestions, to be given only the consideration that is their due.

```
            NORTH
            ♠  10 6 4 2
            ♡  J 3
            ◇  Q 8 6 5
            ♣  A Q 4


            SOUTH
            ♠  A Q 9 8 7 3
            ♡  K 10 8
            ◇  J
            ♣  K 5 3
```

WEST	NORTH	EAST	SOUTH
1 ♡	Pass	2 ♡	2 ♠
Pass	3 ♠	Pass	4 ♠
Pass	Pass	Pass	

West's lead of the diamond ace is followed by the club jack. The ace is taken in dummy, and the spade two led. When East plays the jack you may decide to try the ace, hoping to drop the king; but as there is no particular reason to refuse the finesse, you try the queen. This loses to the king, and the club ten is continued to the king. The last trump is now drawn, ending in dummy, East discarding a diamond. A diamond is ruffed and West drops the king! This may or may not mean anything. You enter dummy with the club queen (on which West plays the eight) and cash the diamond queen, discarding a heart. West shows out, discarding the heart deuce. When you finally get around to playing hearts, the jack is led, getting the inevitable small card from East, who follows with perfect nonchalance.

The rules given previously advise you to play West for the ace and to hope that East has the queen, since West avoided a heart lead. But this time the answer to the question, "Why did they not lead hearts?" is that West has a perfectly normal opening lead in diamonds and, later, had good reason to shift to clubs in which he held at least J-10-8 and, probably, the missing nine. *But* if you reconstruct the hands as they are known to be, a detailed picture emerges. You know that West has two spades, two diamonds, not more than five hearts (since East's showed him to possess the other three) and, therefore, at least four clubs. The hands must look like this:

	WEST		EAST
♠	K 5	♠	J
♡	? x x x x	♡	? x x
◊	A K	◊	10 9 7 4 3 2
♣	J 10 9 8	♣	7 6 2

Had the ace of hearts been with West, the opponents would surely have bid differently. West in all likelihood would have carried on after your two-spade bid; and East, holding not more than 3 high-card points, would not have raised to two hearts in the first place. So the reconstruction should be as follows:

		NORTH		
	♠	10 6 4 2		
	♡	J 3		
	◊	Q 8 6 5		
	♣	A Q 4		

WEST		EAST	
♠ K 5		♠ J	
♡ Q 9 7 6 4		♡ A 5 2	
◊ A K		◊ 10 9 7 4 3 2	
♣ J 10 9 8		♣ 7 6 2	

		SOUTH
	♠	A Q 9 8 7 3
	♡	K 10 8
	◊	J
	♣	K 5 3

So, you correctly play the heart king with confidence. This hand illustrates how the knowledge gained from the actual fall of the cards progressively supplants the tentative probabilities with which the play was begun.

Quiz

NORTH
♠ K Q 7 2
♡ J 7 6 4
◇ J 7
♣ Q J 3

SOUTH
♠ A J 10 5 4
♡ K 2
◇ K 10 6 3
♣ K 7

WEST	NORTH	EAST	SOUTH
1 ♡	Pass	2 ♡	2 ♠
Pass	3 ♠	Pass	4 ♠
Pass	Pass	Pass	

West leads the ace and two of clubs. You take the king and play the ace and king of spades—East-West's spades divide two-two.

You play the club queen, throwing away the heart two as West throws the diamond two. Now what?

1. How many high cards are missing?

2. Does West have both remaining aces?

3. How do diamonds divide?

4. Who has the heart ace?

5. Who has the diamond ace?

6. How do you proceed?

Answers

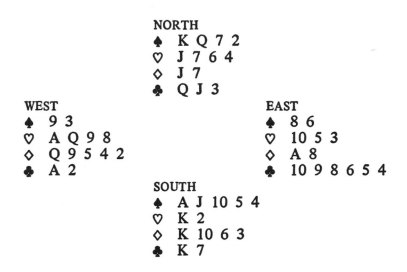

NORTH
♠ K Q 7 2
♡ J 7 6 4
◊ J 7
♣ Q J 3

WEST
♠ 9 3
♡ A Q 9 8
◊ Q 9 5 4 2
♣ A 2

EAST
♠ 8 6
♡ 10 5 3
◊ A 8
♣ 10 9 8 6 5 4

SOUTH
♠ A J 10 5 4
♡ K 2
◊ K 10 6 3
♣ K 7

After West cashed the ace of clubs, you won the club continuation and played spades, ending in dummy. They split two-two. You threw the heart two on the club queen and West discarded the diamond two.

1. You are missing 16 high-card points.
2. West needs at least one of them for his opening bid. If he has them both, then East raised to two hearts on at most two queens. East is probably more likely to have raised with one ace than two queens.
3. West has shown up with two spades, two clubs, and four hearts (East would not raise with two, so he must have three of the outstanding seven hearts). Therefore West has five diamonds and East has four. *two.*

4. West probably has the heart ace for two reasons: First, he might prefer to open one diamond holding four bad hearts and five good diamonds. Second, he might have led a heart from four to the queen rather than the club ace.

5. If all of the previous deductions are true, then East ought to have the diamond ace.

6. Play a diamond to the king and hope that in real life the opponents are as dependable as they are in this book. This is a good point and not intended in jest. The better your opponents, the more confidence you are entitled to vest in deductions similar to these. The worse your opposition, the less you can depend on their bidding and play to guide you.

Dependable means being able to rely on them to follow reasonable lines of bidding or play. A dependable opponent will not do something quite inane. Clearly, at trick two a diamond to the ace and a heart return sets four spades. West in this hand was playing for declarer to hold:

♠ A J 10 5 4
♡ x
◇ K 10 6 3
♣ K 7 x

For whatever reasons West had, he hoped to get one heart, two diamonds (on a misguess) and one club. The club continuation would clearly lose if declarer had:

♠ A J 10 x x
♡ x x
♢ A 10 x x
♣ K x

although this probably is not enough for declarer to go on to game with.

Quiz

NORTH
♠ Q 10 7 6
♡ 9 3
◊ K 5 3
♣ K 6 4 2

SOUTH
♠ A J 8 4 2
♡ K J 2
◊ 7 6
♣ A 10 7

EAST	SOUTH	WEST	NORTH
1 ♡	1 ♠	2 ♡	2 ♠
3 ♡	Pass	Pass	3 ♠
Pass	Pass	Pass	

Opening lead: Diamond ten

1. Who has the diamond ace, queen, and jack?

2. Can West be leading a singleton or a doubleton?

3. Who has the heart ace?

4. Who has the heart queen?

5. Who has the spade king?

If at trick one you play low from dummy, East wins with the jack and returns the heart ten.

6. How do you play?

Answers

                    NORTH
                    ♠ Q 10 7 6
                    ♡ 9 3
                    ◊ K 5 3
                    ♣ K 6 4 2
WEST   EAST
♠ 5 3   ♠ K 9
♡ A 5 4   ♡ Q 10 8 7 6
◊ 10 9 8 4 2   ◊ A Q J
♣ J 9 8   ♣ Q 5 3
                    SOUTH
                    ♠ A J 8 4 2
                    ♡ K J 2
                    ◊ 7 6
                    ♣ A 10 7

1. East clearly has the ace (West would not underlead it), and the jack (West would lead the jack from a J-10 sequence), and probably the queen (why lead an unbid suit headed by the Q-10-9?).

2. No. East cannot have six or seven diamonds, which would be the case if West had only one or two diamonds.

3. West has the heart ace. Why else would West lead a diamond?

4. East has the heart queen except in the unlikely case that West has both the ace and queen of hearts.

5. East probably has the spade king to justify all his bidding.

6. You have to play the heart jack when East makes the heart shift at trick two.

It is barely possible that West has raised with no heart honors. In that case he probably has the spade king and a club honor. But then you were not going to make three spades, so this case does not matter.

Quiz

```
NORTH
♠  J 4 2
♡  10 9 8
◊  K J 10 7
♣  9 8 2


SOUTH
♠  K 8
♡  K Q J 7 6 4
◊  A Q 2
♣  J 4
```

EAST	SOUTH	WEST	NORTH
1 ♠	2 ♡	2 ♠	Pass
Pass	3 ♡	Pass	Pass
Pass			

West leads the club king and then the club three to East's ace. East shifts to the spade five.

1. How many points are you missing?

2. Who has the club queen?

3. Who has the heart ace?

4. Who has the spade ace?

5. Who has the spade queen?

6. Why didn't West lead a spade?

Answers

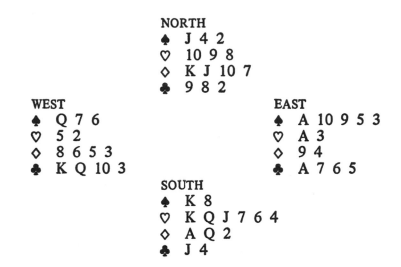

NORTH
♠ J 4 2
♡ 10 9 8
♦ K J 10 7
♣ 9 8 2

WEST
♠ Q 7 6
♡ 5 2
♦ 8 6 5 3
♣ K Q 10 3

EAST
♠ A 10 9 5 3
♡ A 3
♦ 9 4
♣ A 7 6 5

SOUTH
♠ K 8
♡ K Q J 7 6 4
♦ A Q 2
♣ J 4

West leads the club king, winning, and the club three to East's ace. East shifts to the five of spades.

1. You are missing 19 points.
2. West led the king and then led to East's ace. West's lead must have been from the king-queen.
3. East has the heart ace. He needs it to give him an opening bid.
4. East has the spade ace. Same reason.
5. West must have it, as East would not underlead the A-Q of spades.
6. West, holding the spade queen, this time elected not to lead his partner's suit because he had an excellent constructive alternative.

4

Conducting the Investigation

♠ ♡ ◇ ♣

You have already done your thinking about trick one and are now ready to proceed with the hand Sometimes you have no choice in the matter—you must take a finesse, and the key card either is or is not onside. Or you will have to find a suit dividing three-three, and it may or may not divide that way. When things work, you succeed; and when they don't, you don't.

But on many hands you, the declarer, have to make a series of guesses. Sometimes you are able to garner more knowledge than what you learned from the bidding or the opening lead. Or you may be able to develop some clues on hands that started out a mystery (for instance, when the opponents were silent through the auction).

There are two similar techniques for this.

The first is the simple procedure of finding cards by the very act of forcing them to be played. You lead a king, West takes the ace. You have seen West play the ace, and you record the fact that he had it. The play of the ace may be all you need to know regarding the remaining cards. For instance, if West passed originally and then led the ace and king of hearts and subsequently showed up with the club ace, you would be reluctant to credit him with so much as even a jack more. Instead, you would play his partner for all the other missing cards. This chapter will be concerned with this discovery technique only. A description and discussion of a second procedure will follow later.

The first hand is straightforward:

NORTH
♠ A 8 7 4
♡ 10 6 2
◊ J 3
♣ K J 8 7

SOUTH
♠ K Q J 9 2
♡ J 3
◊ K 10 4
♣ Q 10 6

WEST	NORTH	EAST	SOUTH
1 ♡	Pass	2 ♡	2 ♠
Pass	3 ♠	Pass	Pass
Pass			

Opening lead: Heart king

West leads the heart king and ace, then continues with the five. East plays the heart queen, which you ruff. In hands of this nature, where one of your opponents is known to hold a certain range of points, it pays to count the opponents' high cards. Here East has raised one heart to two hearts. This usually shows about 5 to 9 high-card points. After the first three tricks East has shown the heart queen. The remaining outstanding cards are the diamond ace and queen and the club ace. If East has a reasonable raise to two hearts, he is likely to have one of the two aces. The heart queen and the diamond queen only would probably not be worth a response.

After drawing trumps, which divide two-two-, your problem is to discover which ace East has. This is done by playing clubs—the suit in which the location of the ace is immaterial. If

East turns up with the ace of clubs, it is clear that he cannot have the ace of diamonds as well. Play East for the queen of diamonds. If, as in the actual case, West turns up with the club ace, then play East for the diamond ace.

Here is the complete hand:

```
                    NORTH
                    ♠  A 8 7 4
                    ♡  10 6 2
                    ◇  J 3
                    ♣  K J 8 7
    WEST                              EAST
    ♠  10 6                           ♠  5 3
    ♡  A K 8 5 4                      ♡  Q 9 7
    ◇  Q 8 7                          ◇  A 9 6 5 2
    ♣  A 9 2                          ♣  5 4 3
                    SOUTH
                    ♠  K Q J 9 2
                    ♡  J 3
                    ◇  K 10 4
                    ♣  Q 10 6
```

There is a further reason to believe that East has the diamond ace (after you have forced out the club). West might well have bid over two spades had he held:

```
                    ♠  10 6
                    ♡  A K 8 5 4
                    ◇  A 8 7
                    ♣  A 9 2
```

The next hand is similar:

NORTH
♠ A 7 6 4 2
♡ K J
◊ Q 9 6 4
♣ 9 8

SOUTH
♠ 9 3
♡ 5 3
◊ A K 10 8 5 3
♣ K Q 5

WEST	NORTH	EAST	SOUTH
1 ♡	Pass	2 ♡	3 ◊
3 ♡	4 ◊	Pass	Pass
Pass			

West leads the spade king. It is best to win this immediately; if you duck, the inevitable heart shift will come before you are ready to guess it. For the same reason you cannot attempt to set up spades after drawing trumps. West will lead a heart. However it is a moral certainty that West has the ace or queen of hearts, and the only concern is, which one? The answer to this question can be found by leading clubs from the dummy. It is just possible that you may be allowed to throw a heart from dummy on a club (in the event that East has the club ace). In the actual hand, you draw trumps, East having two. A club is led to the king, West takes the ace and shifts to a low heart.

It looks as if East ought to have the heart ace for his raise. Otherwise his high cards would consist of the heart queen and perhaps one or two jacks. This proved to be the case, for the hand was:

```
                    NORTH
                    ♠ A 7 6 4 2
                    ♡ K J
                    ◊ Q 9 6 4
                    ♣ 9 8
WEST                                    EAST
♠ K Q J                                 ♠ 10 8 5
♡ Q 10 9 8 6 2                          ♡ A 7 4
◊ J                                     ◊ 7 2
♣ A 10 7                                ♣ J 6 4 3 2
                    SOUTH
                    ♠ 9 3
                    ♡ 5 3
                    ◊ A K 10 8 5 3
                    ♣ K Q 5
```

Much of the time when you are going to be faced with a guess, it is possible to delay that guess for a few tricks. Usually you can at least draw trumps and scout around a bit in the noncritical side suits.

This hand is such a case:

```
                    NORTH
                    ♠ K 8 7 6 2
                    ♡ 9 4 3 2
                    ◊ K J
                    ♣ Q 7


                    SOUTH
                    ♠ A J 10 5 4 3
                    ♡ A 6
                    ◊ 8 6 3
                    ♣ A 4
```

WEST	NORTH	EAST	SOUTH
1 ♡	Pass	2 ♡	2 ♠
Pass	3 ♠	Pass	4 ♠
Pass	Pass	Pass	

West starts with the heart king. As in the previous example, it is probably best to take this because West may well shift to diamonds before you wish to guess them. You win the opening lead and play one round of trumps, West having the singleton queen and East the nine. It is quite impossible to hope to set up a trick in any suit for a discard, so four spades will require a correct reading in diamonds.

Leading a heart now will not help, as West will surely play diamonds before you learn anything. As you will almost certainly end up losing a club in any case, why not lose it now? After the play of ace and a low club, West is in with the king. The heart queen is cashed, and the diamond ten is led for your inspection. What do you do—and why?

Once again the answer is found by a brief reconstruction of the East and West hands. West has shown up with the king-queen of hearts, the club king, and the spade queen. This leaves East with at most the heart and/or club jacks, and either the ace or queen of diamonds. No combination of these cards seems to justify a raise unless the diamond ace is included. You should therefore play the jack of diamonds and hope to find the cards distributed something like this:

                              NORTH
                              ♠ K 8 7 6 2
                              ♡ 9 4 3 2
                              ◊ K J
                              ♣ Q 7
        WEST   EAST
        ♠ Q   ♠ 9
        ♡ K Q 10 5   ♡ J 8 7
        ◊ Q 10 9 7   ◊ A 5 4 2
        ♣ K J 8 2   ♣ 10 9 6 5 3
                              SOUTH
                              ♠ A J 10 5 4 3
                              ♡ A 6
                              ◊ 8 6 3
                              ♣ A 4

Sometimes you have to do your spade work rather early.

Whereas the preceding hand allowed some time, this one requires immediate attention.

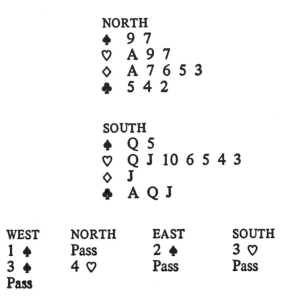

NORTH
♠ 9 7
♡ A 9 7
◊ A 7 6 5 3
♣ 5 4 2

SOUTH
♠ Q 5
♡ Q J 10 6 5 4 3
◊ J
♣ A Q J

WEST	NORTH	EAST	SOUTH
1 ♠	Pass	2 ♠	3 ♡
3 ♠	4 ♡	Pass	Pass
Pass			

Opening lead: Spade king

West leads the king and ace of spades and shifts to the diamond king, which you win. How do you continue? What suit do you play next?

West very likely has either the heart king or the club king. If he has both, then you can win the heart finesse; if East has both, you can win the club finesse. But if they are divided, then you are in danger when West has the club king and East the heart king. So at trick four, before touching trumps, you should take a club finesse. West wins and returns the diamond queen, which you trump. When you lead the heart queen West produces the deuce, and you have to reflect on whether West bid only three spades with:

♠ A K x x x
♡ K x
◊ K Q x
♣ K x x

or, alternatively, if East would raise to two spades with:

♠ J 10 x x
♥ x
♦ x x x x
♣ x x x x

All things considered, you should attempt to drop the heart king offside.

The entire hand:

```
                        NORTH
                        ♠ 9 7
                        ♡ A 9 7
                        ◇ A 7 6 5 3
                        ♣ 5 4 2
        WEST                                    EAST
        ♠ A K 8 6 3                             ♠ J 10 4 2
        ♡ 8 2                                   ♡ K
        ◇ K Q 10                                ◇ 9 8 4 2
        ♣ K 10 3                                ♣ 9 8 7 6
                        SOUTH
                        ♠ Q 5
                        ♡ Q J 10 6 5 4 3
                        ◇ J
                        ♣ A Q J
```

The observant reader may ask what would happen if West were to hold the club king and not take it when the club was led. In practice, very few players would not take the trick if they could, and even fewer would be able to play small without conscious thought. From the defender's point of view, it would often cost a trick to duck, as declarer could have A-Q-x or A-Q alone.

Most of the examples so far have been concerned with locating cards in opponents' hands to justify their bidding. Often, however, you can correctly play a hand after considering bids that were *not* made.

NORTH
♠ K 10 9 7
♡ J 8 2
◇ K 7 2
♣ Q 10 7

SOUTH
♠ A Q 8 2
♡ K Q 7
◇ J 10 9
♣ A 8 2

EAST	SOUTH	WEST	NORTH
Pass	1NT	Pass	2 ♣
Pass	2 ♠	Pass	3 ♠
Pass	4 ♠	Pass	Pass
Pass			

When the dummy comes down it appears that one notrump would have been safer. Your losers include the possibility of a spade, if they do not split, one heart, and perhaps two diamonds and two clubs.

West's lead is the heart five to East's ace. The heart ten is returned, West following with the three. Trumps divide, with East having the doubleton jack. So far so good. Now whatever else happens you need the diamond queen in West's hand to have a play for four spades. So you lead the diamond jack and play low from dummy. More luck is with you as East takes the ace and returns another heart, West discarding a small club. You note that West began with two hearts and East with five. The diamond finesse is repeated, and now all that remains is for you to negotiate a successful guess in clubs. When you play the ace and low in clubs, West of course plays low. A reflection on the play so far shows that East has shown up with something like:

♠ J x
♡ A 10 9 x x
♦ A x x
♣ ? x x

It is not clear whether East has four diamonds and two clubs or three of each, but it looks as though the club king would make this hand worth an opening bid. Play the queen expecting to find this distribution:*

		NORTH		
		♠ K 10 9 7		
		♡ J 8 2		
		♦ K 7 2		
		♣ Q 10 7		
WEST				EAST
♠ 6 5 3				♠ J 4
♡ 5 3				♡ A 10 9 6 4
♦ Q 5 4 3				♦ A 8 6
♣ K 6 5 3				♣ J 9 4
		SOUTH		
		♠ A Q 8 2		
		♡ K Q 7		
		♦ J 10 9		
		♣ A 8 2		

Sometimes even queens can be located with almost 100 percent chance of success.

*It is possible that if East has the doubleton king of clubs he will have to give you a sluff and a ruff.

NORTH
♠ A 9 2
♡ 7 6 4
♢ K 10 4
♣ A Q 10 2

SOUTH
♠ Q 6 5
♡ A 5 2
♢ A J 9
♣ J 9 8 7

WEST	NORTH	EAST	SOUTH
Pass	1 ♣	Pass	2NT
Pass	3NT	Pass	Pass
Pass			

Opening lead: Heart king

West leads the heart king, on which East plays the three. West continues the heart ten, which you duck, followed by the heart queen, which you take. East has showed up so far with the 9-8-3. On playing clubs, you find West to have started with K-6-5, so you are assured of at least eight tricks. If you knew who had the diamond queen, you could take nine. If East has the spade king, you could also take nine tricks. Do you think you can claim your contract now? How?

The play in the heart suit almost certainly marks West with the K-Q-J-10, and he has shown up with the club king. What more can he have? It is quite possible for West to have the spade king or the diamond queen, but not both. You noted, of course, that West dealt and did not open the bidding. With this in mind, you can lead a small spade toward the queen (before cashing the ace) knowing that either the spade queen will win for your ninth trick or, if it loses to the king, it will be a "bridge certainty" that you can successfully play East for the diamond queen.

The full hand was:

```
                        NORTH
                        ♠  A 9 2
                        ♡  7 6 4
                        ◇  K 10 4
                        ♣  A Q 10 2
WEST                                        EAST
♠  K 8 3                                    ♠  J 10 7 4
♡  K Q J 10                                 ♡  9 8 3
◇  8 7 2                                     ◇  Q 6 5 3
♣  K 6 5                                     ♣  4 3
                        SOUTH
                        ♠  Q 6 5
                        ♡  A 5 2
                        ◇  A J 9
                        ♣  J 9 8 7
```

Often you can locate cards with a surprisingly simple but seldom attempted ruse. Here's a little trick that was pulled by my teammate Robert Wolff:

```
                        NORTH
                        ♠  9 8 6 4 2
                        ♡  K 7 6
                        ◇  A Q 8
                        ♣  6 3


                        SOUTH
                        ♠  Q J 10 7 5
                        ♡  A J 5
                        ◇  7
                        ♣  K J 7 4
```

WEST	NORTH	EAST	SOUTH
1 ♡	Pass	1NT	2 ♠
Pass	4 ♠	Pass	Pass
Pass			

West helped things along by starting with the ace and king of trumps; East followed once and then discarded the club two. The shift to the heart ten was equally painless, and Wolff took East's queen with the ace. All of a sudden Wolff had no worries about anything except the club suit. How do you continue against these obliging defenders?

It looks like East has the club ace or the diamond king for his one-notrump bid. How can you find out which it is? You could take a diamond finesse, and if it works you would be fairly certain East had the club ace. But if the diamond finesse lost you would be down, when with another line you might have succeeded.

What can you do to find out what is happening, without unduly jeopardizing your contract? Try this. Take the diamond ace and lead the queen. East will almost surely cover if he has the king. If East covers, you play West for the club ace. If East does not cover, then you assume West has the diamond king and play East for the club ace. In actual play Wolff tried this, and when East played low he trumped the diamond and reentered dummy for a club lead. Wolff, who has never to my knowledge misguessed a queen, correctly played the club king. As he expected, these were the opposing hands:

NORTH
♠ 9 8 6 4 2
♡ K 7 6
◊ A Q 8
♣ 6 3

WEST
♠ A K
♡ 10 9 8 4 2
◊ K 10 9 5
♣ Q 10

EAST
♠ 3
♡ Q 3
◊ J 6 4 3 2
♣ A 9 8 5 2

SOUTH
♠ Q J 10 7 5
♡ A J 5
◊ 7
♣ K J 7 4

The same theme can sometimes be used with a slight extra twist:

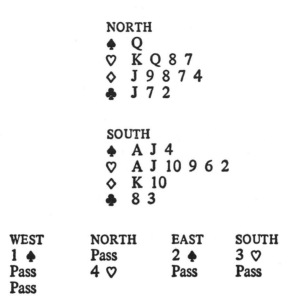

NORTH
♠ Q
♡ K Q 8 7
♦ J 9 8 7 4
♣ J 7 2

SOUTH
♠ A J 4
♡ A J 10 9 6 2
♦ K 10
♣ 8 3

WEST	NORTH	EAST	SOUTH
1 ♠	Pass	2 ♠	3 ♡
Pass	4 ♡	Pass	Pass
Pass			

West leads the king and ace of clubs, East playing the six and five. West continues with the club four to East's queen.

Who has the spade king, the diamond ace, the diamond queen?

Clearly, in order for you to make four hearts, you will need to find East with the diamond ace or queen. And you must guess which one it is. How can you do this? If you could find out if East has the spade king, you would be inclined to play West for the diamond ace to justify his opening bid. On the other hand, if West has the spade king you should probably play East for the diamond ace to justify his raise. How can you find out about the spade king? Does it matter from which hand you first lead spades?

Yes. You should enter dummy with a trump and lead the spade queen. East may cover. If he does not cover, then you take the ace and return the spade jack. West in his turn may cover. If no one plays the king and, in addition, you cannot discern from someone's huddle who has it, then you are playing in the toughest game in town. People are more slaves to habit than you realize, and covering an honor in a seemingly innocuous situation is done as a matter of routine. In the actual hand, West did cover with the spade king and later showed up with a singleton heart. When you lead the diamond jack from dummy, you must ask yourself: "Which is more likely?"

	WEST	EAST
(1)	♠ K 10 7 6 5	♠ 9 8 3 2
	♡ 5	♡ 4 3
	◇ Q 6 3	◇ A 5 2
	♣ A K 9 4	♣ Q 10 6 5

or

	WEST	EAST
(2)	♠ K 10 7 6 5	♠ 9 8 3 2
	♡ 5	♡ 4 3
	◇ A 6 3	◇ Q 5 2
	♣ A K 9 4	♣ Q 10 6 5

You can reasonably play for hand (1), as West might bid over three hearts had he held hand (2),—and East might have passed one spade had *he* held hand (2).

Quiz

NORTH
♠ K 8 7 6 4
♡ 10 9 3
◇ A 9 2
♣ 8 6

SOUTH
♠ A J 10 5 3
♡ K 7 2
◇ K
♣ K J 4 2

WEST	NORTH	EAST	SOUTH
1 ♡	Pass	2 ♡	2 ♠
Pass	3 ♠	Pass	4 ♠
Pass	Pass	Pass	

West leads the diamond queen. West has the singleton spade queen.

1. How many points do the opponents have?

2. Can you tell who has the heart ace?

3. Can you tell who has the club ace?

4. What is the best way to proceed?

Answers

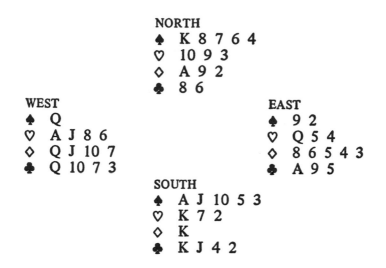

NORTH
♠ K 8 7 6 4
♡ 10 9 3
◊ A 9 2
♣ 8 6

WEST
♠ Q
♡ A J 8 6
◊ Q J 10 7
♣ Q 10 7 3

EAST
♠ 9 2
♡ Q 5 4
◊ 8 6 5 4 3
♣ A 9 5

SOUTH
♠ A J 10 5 3
♡ K 7 2
◊ K
♣ K J 4 2

West leads the diamond queen, which you win, and then shows up with the queen singleton in spades.

1. They have 18 points.
2. & 3. At this point it is not clear who has the missing aces. It looks like East ought to have one of them for his raise. If he does not have an ace, then his raise would have to look like:

♠ x x
♡ Q J x
◊ x x x x
♣ Q x x x

which in turn would give West a heart suit of
A-x-x-x.

4. If you decide East has an ace, the way to proceed
is to discard a heart on the diamond ace and then
lead a heart to the king. If it wins, you are home. If
it loses, well then you are going to lose two hearts
anyway and now you have the option of making
the club guess after you have more information
available. If West leads the heart queen at the next
trick, for instance, you would be sure that East has
the club ace. As it is, you should probably play
him for that card anyway.

Quiz

NORTH
♠ 6
♡ Q 9 6 4
◇ 10 6 5 3
♣ A Q J 2

SOUTH
♠ Q 10 8 3
♡ A J 10 8 7 2
◇ Q
♣ 10 3

WEST	NORTH	EAST	SOUTH
1 ♠	Pass	2 ♠	3 ♡
Pass	4 ♡	Pass	Pass
Pass			

West leads the spade king and shifts to the diamond two.
East plays the ace and returns the diamond four.

1. Who has the spade ace?
2. Who has the diamond king?
3. Who has the heart king?
4. Who has the club king?
5. How do you proceed?

Answers

NORTH
- ♠ 6
- ♡ Q 9 6 4
- ◇ 10 6 5 3
- ♣ A Q J 2

WEST
- ♠ A K 7 4 2
- ♡ K
- ◇ K J 8 2
- ♣ 9 7 4

EAST
- ♠ J 9 5
- ♡ 5 3
- ◇ A 9 7 4
- ♣ K 8 6 5

SOUTH
- ♠ Q 10 8 3
- ♡ A J 10 8 7 2
- ◇ Q
- ♣ 10 3

West leads the spade king, followed by the diamond two to East's ace. East returns the diamond four.

1. West has the spade ace. His opening lead was the king.
2. Probably West has the diamond king.
3. & 4.   It looks like West has one of them. If he had both kings he would have bid over three hearts; if East had both he would have bid more than two spades.
5. Take the club finesse. If it wins you are home. If it loses then you should credit West with the heart king. Hope it is singleton and attempt to drop it.

Quiz

NORTH
♠ A J 8 7
♡ Q 5 4
◇ 8 7 6 2
♣ Q 9

SOUTH
♠ K 10 9 2
♡ K J 10 9 7
◇ 4 3
♣ A 8

SOUTH	WEST	NORTH	EAST
Pass	1 ◇	Pass	1NT
2 ♡	Pass	3 ♡	Pass
Pass	Pass		

West leads the diamond king and queen and continues with the ten to East's ace, which you trump. Your heart lead is allowed to win and the next heart is taken by West, East following. The diamond jack is produced, East playing the club two, and at this point you begin thinking up excuses for making that two-heart bid instead of a takeout double. Then your partner could be playing in spades, and probably wishing you were declaring in hearts. In any case, how do you continue when dummy interrupts your reverie with "It's your play"?

1.   What high cards have shown?

2.   What cards are left?

3.   Who has the spade queen?

4.   How will you proceed?
If you play a third trump, East will discard the club three.

Answers

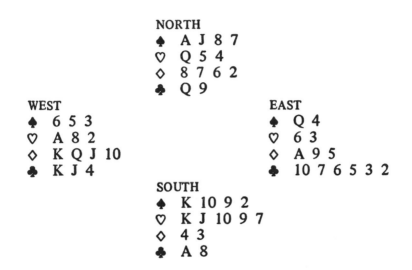

NORTH
♠ A J 8 7
♡ Q 5 4
◊ 8 7 6 2
♣ Q 9

WEST
♠ 6 5 3
♡ A 8 2
◊ K Q J 10
♣ K J 4

EAST
♠ Q 4
♡ 6 3
◊ A 9 5
♣ 10 7 6 5 3 2

SOUTH
♠ K 10 9 2
♡ K J 10 9 7
◊ 4 3
♣ A 8

West leads the king, queen, and ten of diamonds, East playing the ace on the third round. West takes the second heart, East following twice, and plays the diamond Jack. East throws the club two.

1. West: king, queen, jack of diamonds; ace of hearts East; ace of diamonds
2. Spade queen and the king and jack of clubs
3. It could be in either hand.
4. Ruff the diamond and draw the last trump. East probably has the club king or spade queen, so you can proceed thus: club *eight* to the queen. If East has the club king, play West for the spade queen, and vice versa. This works, and you do not have to worry anymore about explanations to partner.

Quiz

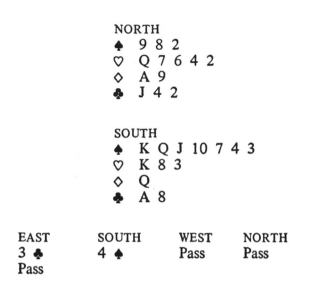

NORTH
♠ 9 8 2
♡ Q 7 6 4 2
◇ A 9
♣ J 4 2

SOUTH
♠ K Q J 10 7 4 3
♡ K 8 3
◇ Q
♣ A 8

EAST	SOUTH	WEST	NORTH
3 ♣	4 ♠	Pass	Pass
Pass			

West leads the club nine, taken with the ace. The spade king goes to East's ace; he cashes the club king, West following with the three, and continues with the queen. Your play.

1.   How many clubs did East have?

2.   Who has the diamond king?

3.   Who has the heart ace?

4.   How do you proceed?

Answers

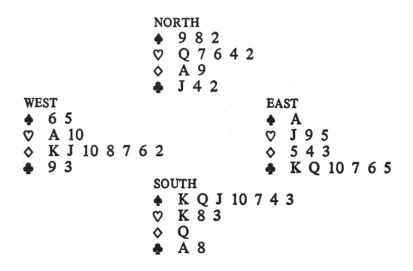

NORTH
♠ 9 8 2
♡ Q 7 6 4 2
◇ A 9
♣ J 4 2

WEST
♠ 6 5
♡ A 10
◇ K J 10 8 7 6 2
♣ 9 3

EAST
♠ A
♡ J 9 5
◇ 5 4 3
♣ K Q 10 7 6 5

SOUTH
♠ K Q J 10 7 4 3
♡ K 8 3
◇ Q
♣ A 8

West leads the club nine to your ace. East takes the first spade and leads the king and queen of clubs, West following to the first.

1. East had six clubs.
2. & 3. West probably has both cards.
4. Trump the club high and draw trump. Lead the diamond queen, and when it is covered take the ace and trump a diamond. Nothing significant happened so you will have to guess the heart suit. Do you think East or West is more likely to have the doubleton ace of hearts. For his preempt East is less likely to have the doubleton ace of hearts, but he is more likely to have a doubleton heart. Which "more likely" do you follow? Probably the better reasoning is to play West for the ace on the theory that East would have opened with one club holding two side aces. Lead a low heart to the queen and duck on the way back.

Quiz

NORTH
♠ 9 8 3 2
♡ Q 8 7 6
◇ A 5 4
♣ J 7

SOUTH
♠ K Q J 10 5 4
♡ K 5 3 2
◇ Q
♣ A 10

WEST	NORTH	EAST	SOUTH
Pass	Pass	3 ♣	4 ♠
Pass	Pass	Pass	

West leads the club three to East's queen and your ace. The diamond queen goes to the king and ace, and a diamond is ruffed with an honor, East following twice. East takes the first spade (the king) and plays the club king, West playing the two. East exits with a spade and West discards a diamond.

1. How many clubs did East have?

2. Who has the heart ace?

3. Does this hand seem familiar?

4. How do you like your chances, and what are your chances?

5. Is the auction the same here as on the previous hand?

Answers

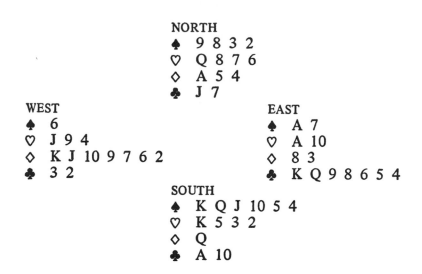

NORTH
♠ 9 8 3 2
♡ Q 8 7 6
◊ A 5 4
♣ J 7

WEST
♠ 6
♡ J 9 4
◊ K J 10 9 7 6 2
♣ 3 2

EAST
♠ A 7
♡ A 10
◊ 8 3
♣ K Q 9 8 6 5 4

SOUTH
♠ K Q J 10 5 4
♡ K 5 3 2
◊ Q
♣ A 10

The club three goes to the queen and ace. The diamond queen is covered by the king and ace, and a diamond is ruffed with an honor, East following twice. The spade king goes to East's ace; he leads the club king, West throwing the two, and exits with a spade. West discards a diamond on this trick.

1. East had seven clubs unless West was doing something strange. West led the three and then followed with the two. This is probably a doubleton.
2. West probably has the heart ace.
3. Yes. Very much like the preceding hand.
4. Your chances are not particularly good. Looking at all the information available to you, you may ask, "What does all this mean?" It means that East has shown up with seven clubs, two spades, at least two diamonds, and therefore two hearts at most. Clearly there cannot be any future in playing West for the doubleton ace of hearts because he *can't* have it, whereas in the last example it was both possible and probable. Your best play is to take

East's lead of the spade in dummy in order to ruff the last diamond, enter dummy again and lead a heart. If East has the singleton or doubleton heart ace, you will succeed.

5.   Yes and no. The auction was different. East opened three clubs in *third* chair, which gives you a slight chance for your contract in that the preempt may have been a bit unusual. Not much of a chance admittedly, but better than going down for sure—which would have happened had you played hearts as in the earlier hand.

Quiz

NORTH
♠ 7 4
♡ K J 9 7 3
◇ J 9 3
♣ J 9 4

SOUTH
♠ K Q J 10 8 5 3 2
♡ A 10 4
◇ K
♣ 10

WEST	NORTH	EAST	SOUTH
1NT*	Pass	2 ◇†	4 ♠
Pass	Pass	Pass	

*16-18 points.
†Natural, signoff.

West leads the king and ace of clubs. You ruff and lead the spade king, which West takes. He leads the club queen. What do you do?

NORTH
♠ 7 4
♡ K J 9 7 3
◊ J 9 3
♣ J 9 4

WEST
♠ A 9
♡ 8 6 2
◊ A 8 4
♣ A K Q 7 2

EAST
♠ 6
♡ Q 5
◊ Q 10 7 6 5 2
♣ 8 6 5 3

SOUTH
♠ K Q J 10 8 5 3 2
♡ A 10 4
◊ K
♣ 10

West leads the king and ace of clubs, which you ruff. West takes the first spade and leads the club queen. Your play.

Questions and Answers:

1. What has West shown up with?
   1. Spade ace and club ace, king, queen.
2. What must West have in addition to give him his one-notrump opening bid?
   2. Missing are the heart queen and the diamond ace and queen. To give West 16 to 18 points, he must have in addition to the 13 points already played, either the diamond ace or both red queens. One queen only makes 15 points, and the ace and one queen add up to 19 points.
3. Should I play the ace and ten of hearts and try to throw away the diamond loser on the heart suit?
   3. This depends on what game you are playing. At match points you might be greedy and attempt this. At rubber bridge you should try to ensure your contract if possible.

4.   Is it possible to ensure my contract?

    4.   Very likely. Trump the club queen, draw the last spade, and lead the diamond king. If West takes it, then East should have the heart queen. West would have 19 points if he had the queen—too much of his one-notrump opening. Conversely, if East has the diamond ace, West will need the heart queen (and the diamond queen) for his opening bid. In return for the loss of an overtrick you have doubled your chance of making four spades. These odds are hard to beat.

Quiz

NORTH
♠ A K Q 2
♡ 9
◇ K J 8 7
♣ 8 7 6 4

SOUTH
♠ 10 9 8 7 6 4
♡ A J 6
◇ 4 2
♣ K 3

WEST	NORTH	EAST	SOUTH
1 ♡	Double	2 ♡	2 ♠
Pass	4 ♠	Pass	Pass
Pass			

West leads the heart king. When you get around to spades, West turns out to have the singleton jack. What are your thoughts? How do you proceed?

```
                        NORTH
                        ♠  A K Q 2
                        ♡  9
                        ◇  K J 8 7
                        ♣  8 7 6 4
WEST                                        EAST
♠  J                                        ♠  5 3
♡  K Q 8 7 5                                ♡  10 4 3 2
◇  Q 10 6                                   ◇  A 9 5 3
♣  A J 5 2                                  ♣  Q 10 9
                        SOUTH
                        ♠  10 9 8 7 6 4
                        ♡  A J 6
                        ◇  4 2
                        ♣  K 3
```

West leads the heart king.

Questions and Answers:

1. How many points am I missing?
   1. 19 points.
2. Who has the missing aces?
   2. Probably each player has one. West might have bid again if he held both, and he needs at least one for his opening bid.
3. After drawing trumps, which suit should be attacked?
   3. Clubs. If East has the ace you are home. If West has it you should play East for the diamond ace and hope West has the queen.

Quiz

```
           NORTH
           ♠  6
           ♡  A 5 4 2
           ◇  A Q J 3
           ♣  A 5 4 2

           SOUTH
           ♠  K 5 3
           ♡  K J 9 8 7 6
           ◇  9
           ♣  K 8 3
```

WEST	NORTH	EAST	SOUTH
Pass	1 ♣	Pass	1 ♡
Pass	2 ◇	Pass	3 ♡
Pass	4NT	Pass	5 ♣
Pass	6 ♡	Pass	Pass
Pass			

Before Robert Hamman joined the team as our sixth, Ira Corn played in many of our matches to give us our full complement of players. Ira has always preached that winning bridge is based on careful analysis and that this cannot be achieved by speeding. Against six hearts, Corn got the lead of the club queen, on which East dropped the ten! Taking the trick with the ace, the heart ace was cashed, dropping West's queen, while East followed. How did Ira continue? And why? One clue—he continued carefully.

```
                        NORTH
                        ♠ 6
                        ♡ A 5 4 2
                        ◊ A Q J 3
                        ♣ A 5 4 2
   WEST                                    EAST
   ♠ A 10 7 2                              ♠ Q J 9 8 4
   ♡ Q                                     ♡ 10 3
   ◊ 10 5 4                                ◊ K 8 7 6 2
   ♣ Q J 9 7 6                             ♣ 10
                        SOUTH
                        ♠ K 5 3
                        ♡ K J 9 8 7 6
                        ◊ 9
                        ♣ K 8 3
```

West led the club queen which was taken with the ace, East dropping the ten. The heart ace was cashed, dropping West's queen with East following. Ira's approach went like this: "I'm going to have to guess who has the diamond king in order to get rid of my club loser." How did he do this?

Questions and Answers:

1. Who has shown up with what cards?
   1. West has the club queen and jack (probably) and the heart queen. West is also a passed hand.
2. If West has the ace of spades, can he also have the diamond king?
   2. No. West passed originally.
3. Shall I lead a spade now toward the king? Am I in any danger?
   3. There is the distinct danger that if West has the ace of spades, East may ruff a club.

4.   Is it necessary for me to get a spade trick?
    4.   No. I can ruff both spade losers in dummy. No discard in dummy will be of any use.
5.   How can I play safely and yet to best advantage?
    5.   Draw the last trump and lead the spade king from your hand! If East takes the trick I'll just have to guess the diamonds as there won't be enough information, but if West wins it . . . .
6.   West did in fact take the trick. Can I claim now?
    6.   Probably. West passed originally and has shown up with the spade ace, heart queen, and club queen (jack). The diamond king would be enough to open the bidding.

Notice that inasmuch as a spade lead from dummy could not be achieved without jeopardizing the contract, it was not tried. Ira's play was just as effective and was 100 percent safe. Once Ira determined that East had the king of diamonds, he led the ace and queen of that suit; and when East did not cover, he discarded his losing club.

5

Checking the Evidence

♠ ♡ ◇ ♣

The second technique for obtaining a further inspection of the opponents' hands before committing yourself to a line of play is the technique of counting.

Counting as used here, however, is not exactly as you may have seen it described in various other texts. The classic example of counting is as follows:

```
            NORTH
            ♠  A Q 8 7
            ♡  Q 9 4
            ◇  K 10 9
            ♣  8 7 3


            SOUTH
            ♠  K J 9 4
            ♡  8 6 2
            ◇  A J 4
            ♣  A K Q
```

NORTH	EAST	SOUTH	WEST
Pass	Pass	1NT	Pass
2 ♣	Pass	2 ♠	Pass
4 ♠	Pass	Pass	Pass

West leads the heart king and ace and gives East a ruff, East having begun with the jack and the seven. The club ten is returned, which you take, and trumps are drawn, West having had two and East three. After cashing your remaining two club honors, you discover that East began with the ten and the two.

Now you can reconstruct West's hand as:

♠ 3 2
♡ A K 10 6 3
◇ ?
♣ J 9 6 5 4

You cash the diamond king, and if West does not play the queen you finesse against East's proven diamond queen.

The hands were:

```
                        NORTH
                        ♠  A Q 8 7
                        ♡  Q 9 4
                        ◇  K 10 9
                        ♣  8 7 3
        WEST                                    EAST
        ♠  3 2                                  ♠  10 6 5
        ♡  A K 10 5 3                           ♡  J 7
        ◇  7                                    ◇  Q 8 6 5 3 2
        ♣  J 9 6 5 4                            ♣  10 2
                        SOUTH
                        ♠  K J 9 4
                        ♡  8 6 2
                        ◇  A J 4
                        ♣  A K Q
```

The above method of counting is used when you are looking for distributional clues to help you locate missing cards. You were trying to locate the diamond queen, hopefully for a certainty as you were able to do here, or at least as a probability—as would happen if you discovered that West had two diamonds and East five in the above hand.

The kind of counting we are going to discuss here, however, is a little different. By playing on an unrelated suit, you may find some information that can assist you in guessing a second suit. The information you get will help you draw inferences such as those made in a preceding chapter.

Let's suppose you have reached this position with spades as trumps. Your problem is to guess the clubs. The opponents' spades have been drawn, and you are in your hand.

```
        ♠  8 7
        ♡  A K 2
        ◊  ——
        ♣  K J

        ♠  A 3
        ♡  4
        ◊  ——
        ♣  10 4 3 2
```

If you have had no help in the bidding, you might lead a club and guess. But suppose you first played off the heart king and ace and trumped the last heart in your hand. If you discovered that East, who had not bid, had seven hearts to the Q-J-10-9-8-7-6, you might decide he would have entered the auction had he held the club ace.

Let's see this idea at work.

```
        ♠  Q 9 8 6 4
        ♡  J 9 7
        ◊  A 8 4 2
        ♣  6


        ♠  A K 10 7 5 2
        ♡  K 10 8
        ◊  9
        ♣  A K 10
```

WEST	NORTH	EAST	SOUTH
Pass	Pass	Pass	1 ♠
Double	Redouble	2 ♣	Double
2 ◊	3 ♠	Pass	4NT
Pass	5 ◊	Pass	6 ♠
Pass	Pass	Pass	

Opening lead: Diamond king

Clearly you like your contract. You throw one of dummy's heart losers on your king of clubs. You can get rid of the other heart loser by playing East for either the ace or queen of hearts. All that is necessary is to guess which one. Of course, if East has neither honor this slam is not going to make anyway. So hope for the best. The first thought is that West should have the heart ace for his double, and unless something happens to indicate otherwise, you should play accordingly.

What could happen to cause you to change your mind? At trick two, trump a diamond in your hand. East, who played the diamond three to the first trick, follows now with the six. A spade to dummy's queen brings the jack from West and the three from East, removing the adverse trumps. Another diamond ruff in your hands gets the seven from East. It is beginning to look as though West has begun with K-Q-J-10-5 of diamonds. When the last club is trumped, West follows with the queen. You can afford to trump the last diamond just to confirm what you already believe. And when East throws a club, it looks like the East-West hands were something like this:

WEST	EAST
♠ J	♠ 3
♡ ? x x x	♡ ? x x
◇ K Q J 10 5	◇ 7 6 3
♣ Q x x	♣ J x x x x x

The fact that West ran from two clubs doubled tends to place him with only three clubs.

After entering dummy with a trump, the heart jack is led and East plays small. Looking at the above hands, the question you should ask yourself "Which is West more likely to have for his bidding?"

♠ J		♠ J
♡ A x x x	or	♡ Q x x x
◇ K Q J 10 5		◇ K Q J 10 5
♣ Q x x		♣ Q x x

It should immediately strike you that if West had the heart ace, his hand would be almost a mandatory opening bid. The correct play then is to put up the heart king. This wins. The exact East-West hands were about what they rated to be after you took the trouble to take a deeper look.

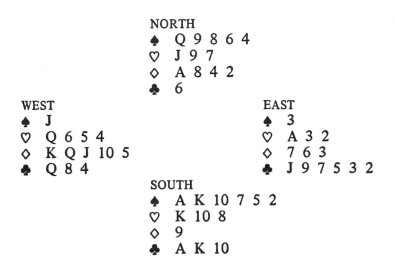

NORTH
♠ Q 9 8 6 4
♡ J 9 7
◊ A 8 4 2
♣ 6

WEST
♠ J
♡ Q 6 5 4
◊ K Q J 10 5
♣ Q 8 4

EAST
♠ 3
♡ A 3 2
◊ 7 6 3
♣ J 9 7 5 3 2

SOUTH
♠ A K 10 7 5 2
♡ K 10 8
◊ 9
♣ A K 10

Some more example hands are given here to show the various kinds of clues available. Usually the information you get is in the nature of distribution, with high cards falling into place accordingly. In the previous hand, when East showed out of diamonds, you also confirmed the high-card location of that suit.

NORTH
- ♠ 7
- ♡ K J 9 5 4
- ◊ A 8 7 6
- ♣ 8 3 2

SOUTH
- ♠ A Q 2
- ♡ A Q 10 8 6 2
- ◊ 5
- ♣ K J 9

EAST	SOUTH	WEST	NORTH
Pass	1 ♡	Pass	3 ♡
3 ♠	4NT	Pass	5 ◊
Pass	6 ♡	Pass	Pass
Pass			

Against six hearts West opens the spade jack, which goes to your queen. The only problem here—the club guess—is very similar to the previous problem. After drawing trumps, which turn out to be divided one-one, you play the diamond ace and ruff the remaining diamonds in your hand. In the process you find that East began with K-Q-2 of diamonds and K-10-9-6-5-4-3 of spades. After throwing one of the dummy's clubs on the spade ace and entering dummy, a club is led, on which East plays the ten. For you to make six hearts, East must have a club honor. Which one? Does East have:

♠ K 10 9 6 5 4 3		♠ K 10 9 6 5 4 3
♡ 3	or	♡ 3
◊ K Q 2		◊ K Q 2
♣ Q 10		♣ A 10

If East had the club ace he would probably have opened the bidding. The play likely to win is the club jack, hoping for East to have the queen and ten.

NORTH
♠ 8 4
♡ A 4 2
◊ K Q 8 7 4
♣ 9 8 2

SOUTH
♠ A Q 10 9
♡ 5
◊ A J 10 9 3 2
♣ K J

SOUTH	WEST	NORTH	EAST
1 ◊	Pass	2 ◊	Pass
2 ♠	Pass	3 ♡	Pass
4 ♣	Pass	5 ◊	Pass
Pass	Pass		

West leads the heart queen. In order to begin an elimination play and possibly get some additional information, you win and ruff a heart. A diamond to dummy finds trumps one-one, and you continue by ruffing the last heart, on which West drops the jack. Dummy is entered with a trump and a spade led to the queen, losing to the king. Now if a club is led you will have to lose only to the club ace; and if West leads a heart, you can throw your club jack on the sluff and ruff. Unfortunately, West has also worked out the problem and he returns a spade, which you win with the ten. The spade ace does not drop the jack. When you ruff your last spade in dummy in order to lead a club, West turns out to have started life with four spades to the king and jack. In spite of all your plans, you are going to have to guess that club suit. When you finally lead that club, East plays the inevitable small card with no hesitation. (He had time to work out the hand, as you should be doing if in his seat.)

What do you play and why? If you have followed the play this far, you will be able to reconstruct the East-West hands without peeking back to the preceding paragraph. All you need recall here is that (1) West led the heart queen and no one has shown out of hearts, (2) diamonds divided one-one, and (3) West had four spades king-jack opposite East's three small.

So West's hand looks like:

> ♠ K J x x
> ♡ Q J x
> ◊ x
> ♣ ? x x x x

Perhaps West was fooling in hearts. It is possible he has four. Just because he played the jack does not mean it was his last card in that suit. But regardless of whether he began with three or four hearts, it is very likely that West could have made a takeout double had he held something similar to:

> ♠ K J x x
> ♡ Q J x
> ◊ x
> ♣ A 10 x x x

Whereas he would surely pass with

> ♠ K J x x
> ♡ Q J x
> ◊ x
> ♣ Q 10 x x x

In any case, the evidence is heavily in favor of rising with the club king. If it loses, just make a note of the apparent conservativeness of West's bidding and make the appropriate allowances in the future.

The first few examples provided fairly strong evidence to guide you to the winning decision. Sometimes, however, after much searching you arrive at a point where you must finally make the crucial guess and it is not clear if the information you have acquired is of any value. Often it pays to have some knowledge of your opponents' habits.

NORTH
♠ A K 8 7
♡ A J 8 2
◇ A 7 6
♣ K J

SOUTH
♠ 9
♡ K Q 10 9 7 6
◇ K Q 8
♣ 10 9 7

You find yourself in six hearts after this auction:

SOUTH	WEST	NORTH	EAST
2 ♡*	Pass	4NT	Pass
5 ♣	Pass	6 ♡	Pass
Pass	Pass		

*Two hearts is a mild preempt showing a decent six-card suit with 6 to 12 high-card points. This is known in tournament circles as the weak two-bid.

West's lead is the spade five. Clearly, your only problem is what to do in clubs. (If you have noticed that you are forever having to guess how to play king-jack opposite some number of small ones—that is not a coincidence. This combination is the most common of those that can wait until you have played out a substantial portion of the hand.) Your approach might be to lead a club as soon as possible, hoping to catch an unwary West before he is ready to make a decision. If West plays small you would probably play the jack on the theory that West did not double five clubs nor did he lead the club ace. Most defenders, however, have become accustomed to this situation, and a good player would have no problem in ducking smoothly when holding the ace. Anyway, the theory that West did not double five clubs and did not lead the club ace—this theory can wait for a few tricks; it won't change.

This hand will be quick to give up any clues it may be hiding. You will be able to play off four rounds of spades and get a complete spade count. Diamonds will yield a complete count unless they divide four-three, in which case you will have to guess who has the thirteenth.

So you proceed and quickly find out that East has started with:

♠ Q J 10 5 4 2
♡ 5 3
♢ J 10 3
♣ ? x x

plus two unidentified cards, which are either the last diamond (the nine) and a club or two clubs. Clearly the odds favor the cards being two clubs. On finally leading the club to the dummy, you must consider if East has

♠ Q J 10 6 4 2		♠ Q J 10 6 4 2
♡ 5 3	or	♡ 5 3
♢ J 10 3		♢ J 10 3
♣ Q x		♣ A x

This is where a knowledge of your opponents habits is so important. If, for example, East is a solid bidder, then you may as well play on the earlier theory that West might have doubled five clubs or led the club ace. But if East likes to bid a lot and, among other things, uses weak two-bids (particularly, if he is of the school that uses them almost willy-nilly) then you should try the club king, playing on the assumption that East would have bid with the second hand. This is very admittedly a vague reason, and if your game does not use weak two-bids, then this case would not apply. But if you do use them and feel competent to judge your opponents' tendencies, then by all means play as your judgment dictates. If your guessing gets you from 50 to 60 percent in this even-money area, it is an extra handful of slams and games made instead of down.

Of such small things are winning decisions made.

Now and then you may be playing a hand out in a logical fashion and something occurs that may cause you to change your line of play from a normal one to a line that at first you would never have considered. What could cause this? Watch. This hand demonstrates how it may happen and how the combined techniques of this and earlier chapters can retrieve an otherwise lost hand. My teammate, Robert Hamman, sat innocently in the South chair in a rubber bridge game and faced this hand. East passed and Bob opened unsuspectingly with one club. The next thing he knew he was in seven clubs after this "racy" auction.

NORTH
♠ A 7 6 5 4
♡ A 4
◇ 3
♣ K Q 9 8 5

SOUTH
♠ 3
♡ 6 3
◇ A Q 10 4
♣ A J 10 7 6 4

EAST	SOUTH	WEST	NORTH
Pass	1 ♣	Pass	1 ♠
Pass	2 ♣	Pass	4NT
Pass	5 ♡	Pass	7 ♣
Pass	Pass	Pass	

The dummy came down and Bob found himself looking at the opening lead of the nine of hearts. His thoughts encompassed, among other things, an urge to strangle partner for one of the worst auctions he had ever heard. On the other hand, the contract was not terrible and, depending on the outcome of the hand, congratulations might be due a nameless partner for a truly fine bid. Can you match Hamman's thoughts as he played the hand?

Seven clubs will succeed if spades divide four-three, in which case you will discard your own losing heart. And it will succeed if East has the diamond king, in which case a finesse will allow you to discard the heart loser from dummy. So, you win the heart ace as East signals violently with the king. In order to keep all the communications between closed hand and dummy alive, you play the spade ace and then ruff a spade. East plays the king and West the queen. This does not look too good for your chances, but it cannot hurt to continue. A club to dummy draws both adverse trumps, and a further spade ruff tells the bad news. West throws the heart five, which means East started with five spades to the K-J-10-9-8. So much for setting up the fifth spade. At least the diamond finesse is still available. Or is it? Who has the diamond king?

East is known to have passed in first seat and has subsequently shown up with K-J-10-9-8 of spades and very likely the K-Q-J-10 of hearts. If East had the diamond king as well, wouldn't he have opened the bidding? So instead you decide to try to drop the diamond king by trumping twice in dummy. So . . . ace of diamonds, ruff a diamond, ruff another spade, ruff a diamond. Right? Wrong! If the diamond king drops from West's hand it will mean he began with this hand.

♠ Q x
♡ ?
◇ K x x
♣ x

He has shown two spades exactly. This diamond holding is what you are hoping for. He has shown one club exactly.

If the spades, diamonds, and clubs are as above, it means the hearts are J-10-9-x-x-x-x. (Remember, East threw the king, so he must have the queen also.) But West led the heart nine. So the hearts cannot be this way. This means West must have more than three diamonds to the king, so the king will not drop when you ruff out the suit. But there is one chance. And that is the possibility that East has the jack of diamonds, which *is* about to drop. If this is the case, you can lead the diamond queen, forcing West to cover. Now if the jack does come down you will make seven clubs, for the diamond ten will become established and the heart loser in dummy discarded. This will be the case if the East-West hands look like this:

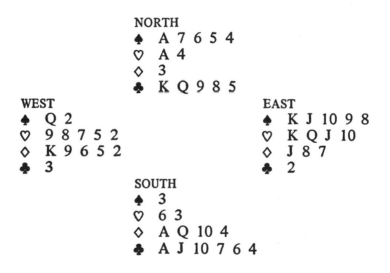

```
                    NORTH
                    ♠  A 7 6 5 4
                    ♡  A 4
                    ◇  3
                    ♣  K Q 9 8 5
  WEST                                      EAST
  ♠  Q 2                                    ♠  K J 10 9 8
  ♡  9 8 7 5 2                              ♡  K Q J 10
  ◇  K 9 6 5 2                              ◇  J 8 7
  ♣  3                                      ♣  2
                    SOUTH
                    ♠  3
                    ♡  6 3
                    ◇  A Q 10 4
                    ♣  A J 10 7 6 4
```

Only by continuous reevaluation of available information was this hand made to succeed. The original plan, good as it was, soon became clearly destined for failure. But by correctly reading what was going on, Hamman was able to negotiate all the traps. (P. S. "That was a wonderful bid, partner. How did you know I had the ten of diamonds?")

One more hand, which combines the above techniques with a little bit of card reading.

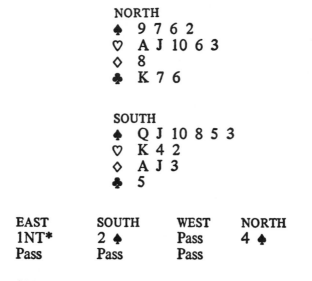

NORTH
- ♠ 9 7 6 2
- ♡ A J 10 6 3
- ◇ 8
- ♣ K 7 6

SOUTH
- ♠ Q J 10 8 5 3
- ♡ K 4 2
- ◇ A J 3
- ♣ 5

EAST	SOUTH	WEST	NORTH
1NT*	2 ♠	Pass	4 ♠
Pass	Pass	Pass	

*15-17 points

West leads the club ten, which is allowed to win, and continues with the club four. Low from dummy fetches the jack, and you ruff. You cannot afford to lead a trump yet as East might be able to lead three rounds of spades in the (admittedly unlikely) event he holds all three.

The diamond ace is followed by a diamond ruff. You enter your hand by trumping the club king, drawing the ace from East, and your last diamond is trumped in dummy. So far no diamond honors have appeared from either side.

Now when dummy leads a spade, East takes the king and ace. West follows with the spade four and then discards a small club. East exits with the club queen, which you trump as West follows suit.

Who has the heart queen? What do you know for sure about the hand so far?

(1) Well, so far you have seen the spade ace and king and the club ace, queen, and jack. This accounts for 14 of East's points.

(2) East must have one of the remaining three outstanding high cards, which are the heart queen and the diamond king and queen.

(3) East can have only one of these high cards. If he had two of them he would have 18 points, which is more than he announced.

If you think West has two of these cards, do you think it is two to one that West has the heart queen? But before you answer that question, go back and review the opening lead. It was a club. What does that mean? How can the club ten have anything to do with the heart queen? In this case it has everything to do with it.

The secret again, as it is so often, is to reconstruct West's hand. It is something along the lines of:

♠ x
♡ ? x
◊ ? ? x x x
♣ 10 9 x x x

The only pertinent point here is to ask what you would have led if you had held:

♠   x
♡   x x
◇   K Q x x x
♣   10 9 x x x

Almost surely the opening lead would have been the diamond king. The fact that it was not led should indicate that West does not have both the king and queen of diamonds. This means West has instead one diamond honor and the heart queen!

NORTH
♠ 9 7 6 2
♡ A J 10 6 3
◇ 8
♣ K 7 6

WEST
♠ 4
♡ Q 7
◇ Q 9 6 4 2
♣ 10 9 8 4 3

EAST
♠ A K
♡ 9 8 5
◇ K 10 7 5
♣ A Q J 2

SOUTH
♠ Q J 10 8 5 3
♡ K 4 2
◇ A J 3
♣ 5

If all these hands seem complicated, just consider that all you have done is to take a "legal peek" into the opponents' hands. Then ask what you could have done with them under varying circumstances as you mentally switch around the one or two missing cards. When they fit—you play accordingly.

Quiz

NORTH
♠ Q 2
♡ Q J 4 3
◇ Q 8 3
♣ Q 7 6 4

SOUTH
♠ A 7 3
♡ A K 10 9 7
◇ 10
♣ K 8 5 2

SOUTH	WEST	NORTH	EAST
1 ♡	Pass	2 ♡	Pass
3 ♡	Pass	4 ♡	Pass
Pass	Pass		

West leads the spade jack. East plays the king on dummy's queen.

1. What is happening in diamonds?

2. What is happening in clubs?

3. What are you going to do, or attempt to do?
If you decide to trump a spade at some point, East will show up with K-9-8-6-5-4 and West with J-10. West has three trumps and East has one.

4. Should you try to get a diamond count?

5. With the information you have, what do you do?

Answers

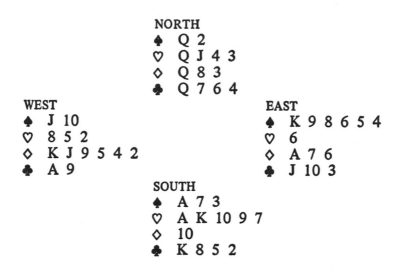

NORTH
♠ Q 2
♡ Q J 4 3
♢ Q 8 3
♣ Q 7 6 4

WEST
♠ J 10
♡ 8 5 2
♢ K J 9 5 4 2
♣ A 9

EAST
♠ K 9 8 6 5 4
♡ 6
♢ A 7 6
♣ J 10 3

SOUTH
♠ A 7 3
♡ A K 10 9 7
♢ 10
♣ K 8 5 2

West leads the spade jack, which is covered by the queen and king.

1. West does not have the ace and queen of diamonds. East therefore has at least one of them.
2. As East is marked with the spade king and a diamond honor, you should tentatively be inclined to play West for the club ace.
3. Get some sort of count on the opponents' distribution.
4. No. Getting a diamond count would mean trumping twice in your hand. This would run you out of trumps, and whoever has the club ace will be able to run whatever suit he has left.

5. Finding East with six spades to the king and the
    hypothetical diamond honor more or less confirms
    the original idea that West has the club ace. Play to
    the queen and duck on the way back. Only if East
    counted out for a doubleton club would you play
    him for the doubleton ace of clubs. You would do
    this if he showed up with something like this:

    ♠ K 10 x x x x x
    ♡ x x
    ◇ A x
    ♣ ? x

    Even though it would be hard to believe East could
    have the club ace along with his other cards, you
    would have to hope he did in fact have it, having
    succumbed to a bout of timidity. If you know a
    suit divides in a certain fashion, then you must
    pretend the cards are distributed within that
    framework to your advantage. If you cannot
    succeed unless someone has psyched, then assume
    it is so. In this case you would have to assume that
    East passed with:

    ♠ K 10 x x x x
    ♡ x x
    ◇ A x
    ♣ A x

But if you knew for a fact that the East had exactly two clubs, then you should proceed on the assumption that East is Mr. Conservative himself.

Quiz

NORTH
♠ 10 3 2
♡ K 9 6 4
◇ A Q 2
♣ Q 8 4

SOUTH
♠ K Q
♡ A Q 10 8 7 2
◇ 5 3
♣ K 10 3

NORTH	EAST	SOUTH	WEST
Pass	Pass	1 ♡	Pass
3 ♡	Pass	4 ♡	Pass
Pass	Pass		

West leads the spade nine to East's ace. East returns the spade seven and West follows with the six.

If you elect to draw trumps now, West will show up with the singleton jack, East having the five and three.

1. If you draw trumps, in which hand do you finish? And what is your play now?

2. If you trumped the last spade, West shows out. What now?

3. The diamond finesse lost and East returned the diamond ten. What now?

4. East followed to the third diamond. What is his distribution and what cards does he have?

5. You have to guess the clubs now. How would you play them normally?

6. Do you have any reason not to do the normal thing? Why? What will you do?

Answers

```
                    NORTH
                 ♠  10 3 2
                 ♡  K 9 6 4
                 ◇  A Q 2
                 ♣  Q 8 4
WEST                                EAST
♠  9 6                              ♠  A J 8 7 5 4
♡  J                                ♡  5 3
◇  J 9 8 6 4                        ◇  K 10 7
♣  A J 7 5 2                        ♣  9 6
                    SOUTH
                 ♠  K Q
                 ♡  A Q 10 8 7 2
                 ◇  5 3
                 ♣  K 10 3
```

West leads the spade nine to the ace, and the seven is returned to your king, West following with the six.

1. Draw trump ending in dummy. Ruff the last spade. Make note of the fact that West discards a small club.
2. Finesse the diamond. This loses, unfortunately, and East returns the diamond ten.
3. Ruff the last diamond. East follows with the seven.

4.   East has:

♠	A J 8 7 5 4		♠	A J 8 7 5 4
♡	5 3	or	♡	5 3
◇	K 10 7		◇	K 10 7 ?
♣	? ?		♣	?

5.   Normally you would lead a club to the queen and then finesse the ten later.

6.   Definitely. You know West has at least five clubs and therefore he is very likely to have the club jack. Your best play is to go to dummy with a trump and lead a small club to the king! If West takes the ace he will have to lead a club, hopefully and probably from the jack, or he will have to give you a sluff and a ruff. Only if East has the jack doubleton of clubs will you lose by this line. If East has the ace of clubs (and he won't in practice, or he would have bid), then it will fall on the next lead of clubs.

Quiz

NORTH
♠	7 2
♡	A 10 8 6 4
◇	Q 10 8
♣	A K 3

SOUTH
♠	A K 4
♡	Q J 9 7 3
◇	A 6 2
♣	10 5

After a one-heart bid by you and a pass by West, your partner took you by the hand and proceeded for some reason to embalm you in a final contract of six hearts. The fact that this spot isn't hopeless, as far as your partner's bidding was concerned, is merely accidental. In any case, the starting card is the spade queen.

1. How bad is this contract?

2. Do you take the heart finesse?

3. What plans do you have if the heart finesse works with East following suit?

4. If you eliminated the clubs and hearts and spades, West would show up with

♠ Q J 10 x x x		♠ Q J 10 x x x
♡ K x	or	♡ K x
◇ ? ?		◇ ?
♣ Q J x		♣ Q J x ?

What conclusions do you draw from this?

5. What is your line of play now?

Answers

NORTH
♠ 7 2
♡ A 10 8 6 4
◇ Q 10 8
♣ A K 3

WEST
♠ Q J 10 8 5 3
♡ K 5
◇ 5 3
♣ Q J 2

EAST
♠ 9 6
♡ 2
◇ K J 9 7 4
♣ 9 8 7 6 4

SOUTH
♠ A K 4
♡ Q J 9 7 3
◇ A 6 2
♣ 10 5

Against your six-hearts contract West leads the spade queen.

1. Only poor. It takes a heart finesse and a guess in diamonds.
2. Yes. There is no particular reason not to.
3. Draw trumps and ruff out the spades and clubs. Perhaps there may be a clue.
4. There is a clue! From the elimination comes the information that West has a hand something like:

    ♠ Q J 10 x x x
    ♡ K x
    ♦ ? ?
    ♣ Q J x

   From this you might decide West does not have the diamond king.
5. Play a small diamond from your hand and insert the ten from dummy. East will win with the king, in which case you have made six hearts. Or East will win with the jack, in which case he will be endplayed if he has the diamond king. He will have to give a sluff and a ruff or lead from the king, either of which will suit you fine. This play loses only if West has the king and one small diamond and plays low smoothly when you lead toward the dummy. Notice that the ace and then small in diamonds loses the contract on this hand.

6

Nailing Down the Case

♠ ♡ ◇ ♣

Every now and then at the bridge table, one of your opponents plays a suit in what appears to be an unusual manner. Perhaps he attempts to drop a king when missing four cards in a suit, rather than take a percentage finesse. Or perhaps your opponent plays the hand as if he assumed you were the person holding the spade king rather than your partner, in spite of the fact that your partner opened the bidding with one spade.

One of the hands you remember so well is this one. You sat West. The auction was opened with one club by your partner, East. That was the end of your side's bidding as the opponents quickly reached four spades.

```
                    NORTH
                    ♠  A 6 4
                    ♡  K 8 7 6 5 3
                    ◇  8 3
                    ♣  Q 5
WEST                                    EAST
♠  K 5 2                                ♠  3
♡  Q 10 9                               ♡  A J
◇  9 6 5 4                              ◇  J 10 7 2
♣  10 9 7                              ♣  A K J 6 4 3
                    SOUTH
                    ♠  Q J 10 9 8 7
                    ♡  4 2
                    ◇  A K Q
                    ♣  8 2
```

123

After your lead of the club ten, the suit was continued. Declarer took the diamond shift at trick three and led the spade queen (which you wisely did not cover) and instead of finessing went up with the ace.

When this apparently unusual play did not work, you were happy to accept the defeat of the contract by what seemed to be more tricks than were necessary. And you may even have chortled a bit as you pointed out that the normal finesse would have saved a trick.

But then a funny thing happened. Later in the evening this rather familiar hand came up.

```
                        NORTH
                        ♠  A 6 4
                        ♡  K 8 7 6 5 3
                        ◇  8 3
                        ♣  Q 5
        WEST                                EAST
        ♠  5 3 2                            ♠  K
        ♡  A 10 9                           ♡  Q J
        ◇  9 6 5 4                          ◇  J 10 7 2
        ♣  10 9 7                           ♣  A K J 6 4 3
                        SOUTH
                        ♠  Q J 10 9 8 7
                        ♡  4 2
                        ◇  A K Q
                        ♣  8 2
```

The bidding was also familiar. One club by East, a one-spade overcall by South, after which four spades was reached. Two rounds of clubs were played, followed by a diamond shift. Declarer won and led the spade queen. Again when you failed to produce the king and the ace was played from dummy. This time the king fell, and later declarer led toward the heart king.

When the heart king turned out to be a winner, declarer claimed his rather lucky contract.

Naturally, under these conditions you suspected something was afoot. Declarer could not have been peeking because you and your partner always protect against that eventuality. A furtive look around the room finds no mirrors or cameras, and the declarer's wife has been in the kitchen for the last ten minutes. You remember that you shuffled the deck and that you purchased the cards yourself just prior to the game.

So with more than the usual curiosity you ask declarer which school of occultism he attends. This question got you back your previous chortle with quite a bit to spare. You also got an explanation that sounded something like this:

"In order for me to make my contract, I must find you with the ace of hearts. I can't succeed if your partner has the ace. If in fact you do have the ace, I cannot believe you can also have the king of spades, for then you might have responded after your partner opened the bidding. Therefore I had to assume the king was in your partner's hand, and I needed to find it singleton, which in fact it was"

What happened to you here was not particularly mysterious. It was just that your opponent took advantage of a frequently recurring bridge situation that is seldom recognized. It is called "card placing by assumption." In some circles it is called "wishful thinking." This form of card placing (henceforth called CPA) is much simpler than its long name might make it sound. In fact it is almost exactly like the card placing discussed in the first chapter, but with one major difference. Learn this properly and you may discover a whole new world of bridge. The cards will sit up and speak to you as friends, not as strange designs on the backs of the pasteboards being clenched furiously by your ill-wishing opponents.

This is the difference: *Rule*—When you cannot make a contract unless a certain card is in a certain place, then assume it is where it must be and play the hand accordingly. You may find that on occasions you go down an extra trick, but if you look at the hand you will see that you could not have made your contract in any case.

Look again at the first hand from this chapter:

```
                        NORTH
                        ♠ A 6 4
                        ♡ K 8 7 6 5 3
                        ◇ 8 3
                        ♣ Q 5
        WEST                            EAST
        ♠ K 5 2                         ♠ 3
        ♡ Q 10 9                        ♡ A J
        ◇ 9 6 5 4                       ◇ J 10 7 2
        ♣ 10 9 7                        ♣ A K J 6 4 3
                        SOUTH
                        ♠ Q J 10 9 8 7
                        ♡ 4 2
                        ◇ A K Q
                        ♣ 8 2
```

Declarer played in four spades after a club opening bid by
East. After the defense took two clubs and shifted to a
diamond, South tried to drop the spade king. This did not
work, and obviously the finesse would have saved a trick. But
had the spade finesse worked, then the heart ace was clearly
marked with East, and four spades would be down even though
there were no spade losers.*

This principle is so important it will warrant many
examples. Look at these two North-South hands side by side.
They are fairly similar in appearance but each requires a
different approach.

In both hands the bidding has been:

WEST	NORTH	EAST	SOUTH
Pass	Pass	Pass	1 ♠
Pass	2 ♠	Pass	Pass

*It is possible that East could have a singleton heart ace, but that would
be less likely than a singleton spade king and would mean West had
Q J 10 9 of hearts. He might have led one.

West has led the heart king followed by the queen and the ten to East's ace. East returns a small club. What do you play from each hand? Why?

NORTH
♠ K 10 9 6
♡ J 5 4
◊ K 8 5 4
♣ 7 6

SOUTH
♠ A Q J 7 4
♡ 9 3 2
◊ J 9
♣ K J 10

NORTH
♠ K Q 10 9
♡ J 5 4
◊ J 4 3 2
♣ 7 6

SOUTH
♠ A J 7 6 4
♡ 9 3 2
◊ Q
♣ K J 10 3

You would like to know who has the diamond ace because with all the other high cards that have shown up you probably could tell who had the club ace. But here you will not be able to find out about the diamond suit until later, and you have already been forced into the club guess. What will guide you? This hand is a classic case of CPA. You have lost three heart tricks and will surely lose to both the club and diamond aces. In order for two spades to make, the diamond-suit losers must be held to one; this can occur only if West has the diamond ace. So mentally say to yourself, "West has the diamond ace," and proceed.

West has shown up with the diamond ace (hopefully,

This time the only concern is how to play the club suit. You do not care how any other suit is located, so it is not necessary to "place" cards. All that is needed is to ascertain as best as possible (Chapter Two) what is actually happening.

West has shown up with the heart king and queen, and because neither defender has led a diamond it looks like West also has the diamond ace or king. The club ace in West's hand in addition to the other high cards (proven and probable) would have given him reason to open the bidding or perhaps to make a passed-hand takeout double. His silence should deny the club ace, and the correct play is the king of clubs.

by CPA) so therefore he cannot have the club ace as well.
You play the club king and it
wins.

These are the adverse
cards.

In both this hand and the
companion hand the winning
play was the club king. But in
one case an assumption was
made while in the other only
facts and reasonable probabilities were used.

These were the adverse
cards.

```
            NORTH                        NORTH
          ♠ K 10 9 6                   ♠ K Q 10 9
          ♡ J 5 4                      ♡ J 5 4
          ◊ K 8 5 4                    ◊ J 4 3 2
          ♣ 7 6                        ♣ 7 6

WEST              EAST           WEST              EAST
♠ 8 5             ♠ 3 2          ♠ 8 5             ♠ 3 2
♡ K Q 10          ♡ A 8 7        ♡ K Q 10          ♡ A 8 7 6
◊ A 7 6 2         ◊ Q 10 3       ◊ A 9 6 5         ◊ K 10 8 7
♣ Q 5 4 2         ♣ A 9 8 3      ♣ Q 8 4 2         ♣ A 9 5

          SOUTH                        SOUTH
          ♠ A Q J 7 4                  ♠ A J 7 6 4
          ♡ 9 3 2                      ♡ 9 3 2
          ◊ J 9                        ◊ Q
          ♣ K J 10                     ♣ K J 10 3
```

Notice that if the club
king had lost to the ace, then
the diamond ace would certainly have been with East. In
that case you would have been
down anyway. By playing as
you did you are catering to
the distribution that would
allow two spades to make
when it could.

It appears the opponents
were very conservative, and
even with the cards as they
were, some more aggressive
players would have been bidding. That, however, is their
concern and not ours.

Throughout these hands you must not lose sight of the rule: "When a card must be properly located for you to succeed, then assume it to be so and play accordingly."

NORTH
♠ K J 5 4
♡ 8 7 2
◊ 8 6 3
♣ K J 8

SOUTH
♠ 7 3
♡ K Q 5
◊ Q 9
♣ A Q 10 9 7 2

WEST	NORTH	EAST	SOUTH
1 ◊	Pass	1 ♠	2 ♣
Pass	Pass	2 ◊	Pass
Pass	3 ♣	Pass	Pass
Pass			

West leads the diamond king and ace, East following with the four and ten. West continues with the spade ten. This is a fairly common situation for CPA. Your losers are two diamonds, one heart for sure, and one spade for sure, with excellent chances of losing additional tricks in either hearts or spades. The card that you must "assume to be somewhere" is the heart ace. This must be in East's hand—otherwise you will have to lose two hearts against good defense. Proceeding on this assumption, it should be clear that West will need the ace of spades for his opening bid. Therefore you go up with the king, knowing that if East has the ace, three clubs is going down to defeat anyway.

This is the complete hand:

```
                        NORTH
                        ♠ K J 5 4
                        ♡ 8 7 2
                        ◊ 8 6 3
                        ♣ K J 8
        WEST                                    EAST
        ♠ A 10                                  ♠ Q 9 8 6 2
        ♡ J 9 6 4                               ♡ A 10 3
        ◊ A K 7 5 2                             ◊ J 10 4
        ♣ 6 4                                   ♣ 5 3
                        SOUTH
                        ♠ 7 3
                        ♡ K Q 5
                        ◊ Q 9
                        ♣ A Q 10 9 7 2
```

This was very good defense by West, because he forced you to make a decision before you wanted to commit yourself. If West had quietly led a third diamond, you would have had plenty of time to test the hearts before deciding how to play spades.

An interesting sidelight to this hand would have occurred had the cards been distributed in this manner:

```
                        NORTH
                        ♠ K J 5 4
                        ♡ 8 7 2
                        ◊ 8 6 3
                        ♣ K J 8
        WEST                                    EAST
        ♠ Q 10                                  ♠ A 9 8 6 2
        ♡ A 10 6 4                              ♡ J 9 3
        ◊ A K 7 5 2                             ◊ J 10 4
        ♣ 6 4                                   ♣ 5 3
                        SOUTH
                        ♠ 7 3
                        ♡ K Q 5
                        ◊ Q 9
                        ♣ A Q 10 9 7 2
```

If the defense had gone the same way—*i.e.*, ace and king of diamonds followed by the spade ten—declarer would go up with the spade king as we have seen because it offers the best chance to make three clubs. On this hand, however, it means you will be down two instead of down one. East wins the spade and switches to hearts before you can develop a spade trick as a discard for your heart loser. Again West would have to make a good play. If a spade was not played right now, declarer would find that the heart ace was offside. Now when a spade is led, declarer is no longer concerned with improving his chances to make his contract, but is just trying for an educated guess to go down one instead of two.

NORTH
♠ K Q 10 4
♡ 10 7 3
◇ A J 10
♣ K J 2

SOUTH
♠ A J 9 7 6 3
♡ Q 6
◇ Q 8 4
♣ 8 6

WEST	NORTH	EAST	SOUTH
1 ♡	Double	2 ♡	3 ♠
Pass	4 ♠	Pass	Pass
Pass			

Against your four spades West takes the ace and king of hearts before shifting to the ten of clubs. Here the crucial CPA card is the king of diamonds: four spades depends on finding it with West. So assume that West has it, and then decide which one of the following hands East has for the raise to two hearts.

(a) ♠ x x
     ♡ J x x
     ◇ x x x
     ♣ Q x x x x

(b) ♠ x x
     ♡ J x x
     ◇ x x x
     ♣ A x x x x

(c) ♠ x   or   (d) ♠ x
    ♡ J x x   ♡ J x x
    ◇ x x x x   ◇ x x x x
    ♣ A x x x x   ♣ Q x x x x

I would expect most opponents to have hand (b). It is not even proved that East has the heart jack. It well might be with West, which greatly increases the chances of East having hand (b). Your best play here to maximize the chances of making four spades is to play the club jack. This works, because this was the distribution:

```
                    NORTH
                    ♠ K Q 10 4
                    ♡ 10 7 3
                    ◇ A J 10
                    ♣ K J 2
    WEST                            EAST
    ♠ 2                             ♠ 8 5
    ♡ A K 9 5 2                     ♡ J 8 4
    ◇ K 9 7 3                       ◇ 6 5 2
    ♣ Q 10 4                        ♣ A 9 7 5 3
                    SOUTH
                    ♠ A J 9 7 6 3
                    ♡ Q 6
                    ◇ Q 8 4
                    ♣ 8 6
```

Now that a number of hands have been studied, we can take a look at another pair of hands that may at first seem alike. Each requires a different approach, however, and the problem is to use the applicable logic.

In both cases the bidding has been:

WEST	NORTH	EAST	SOUTH
Pass	Pass	Pass	1 ♠
2 ♣	2 ♠	3 ♣	4 ♠
Pass	Pass	Pass	

NORTH
♠ A 5 2
♡ 8 6 4
◊ K J 7 6 3
♣ 7 2

SOUTH
♠ K Q J 10 9 7 6
♡ K 5
◊ 8
♣ A 9 3

NORTH
♠ A 5 2
♡ 8 6 4
◊ K J 7 6
♣ 10 7 2

SOUTH
♠ K Q J 10 9 7 6
♡ A 7 5
◊ 8
♣ A 5

Against your four-spade game, West has led the club queen. You allow this to win because you would prefer, if possible, to keep East off lead. A heart shift could be embarrassing and, for the time being at least, it can be avoided. West continues with the club jack, which you win. Trumps are drawn—West has two and East one. The diamond eight is led toward dummy and West plays low.

Do you play the king or the jack? Why?

Against what may by now seem to be a rather familiar four-spade contract by you, West starts off with the heart king. East plays the two and you decide to allow the king to hold. West continues with the heart jack, which you take. Trumps are drawn in two rounds, with West having a doubleton and East a singleton. Now the diamond eight is led toward the dummy and it is your play again when West plays low. Do you play the king or the jack? Why?

One or two things here are clear-cut:

(1) If the East has the heart ace you will always make four spades.

(2) If East has the diamond ace as well as the club king, which seems to be marked by the opening lead, then West's overcall places the heart ace in his hand.

If you played the jack of diamonds then one of two things happened:

(1) It is lost to the queen, in which case nothing was gained and you will still have to find the heart ace with East; or

(2) The jack forced the ace, providing you with a heart discard. Unfortunately, however, East has returned a heart and you know as well as I do that you are going to lose two hearts before you can use the nice king of diamonds.

If you played the king of diamonds, one of two things happened:

(1) East took the ace and has returned a heart, in which case four spades was always going to go down; or

(2) The king won and four spades is now cold. You may even make an overtrick if East has the heart ace.

This time you are faced with a guess similar to that in the accompanying hand. You must guess right inasmuch as you will not have any further options should you be wrong.

Here, however, there are no extra considerations to confuse the issue. All that need be done is to glance at the facts already accumulated with no concern for additional things that "must" or "must not" happen.

The reasoning here is straight out of an earlier chapter.

You know West is a passed hand and he has already shown up with the king, queen, and jack of hearts (unless he led from king, jack alone). West also has some kind of club suit that was worth an overcall. Five to the queen-jack or five to the king-jack is about as bad as it is likely to be. If West had the diamond ace in addition to these cards, then he would have opened the bidding.

It is not at all unreasonable to play East for the diamond ace, instead of the overcaller, and the right play here is almost always going to be the jack, hoping to find the cards distributed something like this:

This is the complete hand:

```
              NORTH                        NORTH
              ♠ A 5 2                      ♠ A 5 2
              ♡ 8 6 4                      ♡ 8 6 4
              ◇ K J 7 6 3                  ◇ K J 7 6
              ♣ 7 2                        ♣ 10 7 2

WEST            EAST              WEST            EAST
♠ 8 4           ♠ 3              ♠ 8 4           ♠ 3
♡ A 10 2        ♡ Q J 9 7 3      ♡ K Q J 3       ♡ 10 9 2
◇ A 5 4         ◇ Q 10 9 3       ◇ Q 5           ◇ A 10 9 4 3 2
♣ Q J 10 8 5    ♣ K 6 4          ♣ K J 9 4 3     ♣ Q 8 6

              SOUTH                        SOUTH
              ♠ K Q J 10 9 7 6             ♠ K Q J 10 9 7 6
              ♡ K 5                        ♡ A 7 5
              ◇ 8                          ◇ 8
              ♣ A 9 3                      ♣ A 5
```

As can be seen from the diagram, it was a good idea to duck the opening lead. If the club ace had been taken at the first trick, East would have been able to gain entry with the club king (assuming West rose with the diamond ace) to make the killing heart return.

The important point of this hand is the realization that if East had the diamond ace you were probably going down. Your play catered to the hand that actually existed and gave you a chance to succeed whenever possible.

About the only time the jack turns out to be wrong is when West forgot to open the bidding with a good hand or when he decided to overcall on some very poor club suit.

Every now and then you will come upon a hand that requires more than a normal number of assumptions. This does not occur too often, but when it does happen, your chances of playing correctly will be increased greatly by following the correct logic.

It is one of bridge's more satisfying moments, incidentally, to play one of these hands and succeed because you used the right reasoning.

Robert Goldman, one of my quieter teammates, played this hand some months ago. I am afraid that I might never have seen it had I not been dummy at the time, as Bobby is not one to discuss hands.

NORTH
♠ K 7
♡ A K 4 2
♢ 10 9 6 5
♣ J 10 8

SOUTH
♠ J 4
♡ 8 5 3
♢ A Q J 4
♣ A Q 9 7

EAST	SOUTH	WEST	NORTH
Pass	1 ♢	Pass	1 ♡
Pass	1NT	Pass	2NT
Pass	3NT	Pass	Pass
Pass			

Against this sequence West led the inevitable small spade, the deuce. What do you play at trick one? Do you think it matters? You might play the king hoping West has led from the ace, or you might play the seven hoping West has led from the queen.

How do the spades divide? Who has the long spades? What are your chances of making three notrump and, specifically, what must happen for you to succeed?

In some way or another it is important to have answered, or at least to have considered, all these questions. Robert Goldman reasoned the hand this way.

"For me to make three notrump I will have to take winning finesses in clubs and diamonds. This will be the case only if East has both minor-suit kings. I will therefore assume that these cards are in fact with East. Furthermore, I see that West has led the spade two. Unless West is false-carding me, I can reasonably expect to find East with a five-card spade unit.

"What do I know from the bidding? East passed originally, which does not mean much, but then he passed again after my partner's one-heart response. It seems to me that if East had been looking at five spades to the ace, and both kings (which I am assuming), then he might well have bid one spade after having passed earlier." With all of these considerations in mind, Goldman played the spade king at trick one and was rewarded when the hands proved to be:

```
                    NORTH
                    ♠  K 7
                    ♡  A K 4 2
                    ◇  10 9 6 5
                    ♣  J 10 8
    WEST                                EAST
    ♠  A 10 6 2                         ♠  Q 9 8 5 3
    ♡  Q J 7                            ♡  10 9 6
    ◇  8 7 2                            ◇  K 3
    ♣  6 4 2                            ♣  K 5 3
                    SOUTH
                    ♠  J 4
                    ♡  8 5 3
                    ◇  A Q J 4
                    ♣  A Q 9 7
```

This proved to be a lucky hand, but nonetheless a well-played one. Its success depended on finding both kings onside and guessing which spade to play at trick one. All in all, it came to around one chance in eight, or about 13 percent.

Had South instead decided to play low at trick one and found that East had the spade ace instead of the queen, then his chances of finding both missing kings with East would have diminished considerably. My guess would be that what was a 13 percent chance to make by playing the king at the first trick would now be diminished to about 7 percent by ducking the opening lead.

Goldman's play of the king, it seems to me, almost doubled his admittedly slim chance.

Here is another case that follows the same theme as the preceding hand. Before you continue with the discussion you might look at the conditions and see if you can come up with the same winning line as did Jim Jacoby. It is important that you see why you play as you do. If you are not sure of your reasons, look again at the last hand before going on to the answer below.

NORTH
♠ Q 10
♡ A K Q J
◇ 9 7
♣ J 9 7 6 5

SOUTH
♠ A 7
♡ 10 8 7 6 5 3 2
◇ K 5
♣ K 2

Both sides vulnerable

EAST	SOUTH	WEST	NORTH
Pass	Pass	Pass	1 ♣
1 ♠	2 ♡	3 ♠	Pass
Pass	4 ♡	4 ♠	5 ♡
Pass	Pass	Pass	

Opening lead: Spade three

You certainly do not have to approve of the bidding, and I am sure Jim was not ecstatic with his chances of making five hearts when the dummy came down. However, Jim is not in the habit of going down when something better is available, and he settled down to see what he could do to make the most of his chances. Jim reasoned: "Clearly it will be necessary to make the correct guess in spades right now at trick one. Is West's lead from the king or from the jack? And even if I guess right, what will I need to bring this home? Can this contract be made if West has either of the minor-suit aces? No. Therefore I will assume East, who has overcalled one spade after originally passing, has both aces. Can he also have the spade king, or is he more likely to have overcalled on a jack-high suit? I think that if East has the two aces I want him to have, I shall be inclined not to play him for the spade king. With that card East might have opened the bidding. In addition I have no reason to believe he doesn't have some extra lesser card like the club queen or the diamond queen or jack."

So Jim played the spade queen at trick one, in spite of the fact that East had bid spades. He did not play the spade queen because he thought it would win but because he knew that if East had the spade king, he (South) was most unlikely to succeed in any case. Only if the spade king was with West would the minor suit aces both be in the East hand.

It appears that Jacoby's efforts were well spent, for his wishes came true:

NORTH
♠ Q 10
♡ A K Q J
♦ 9 7
♣ J 9 7 6 5

WEST
♠ K 8 6 3
♡ —
♦ Q 8 6 3 2
♣ Q 10 4 3

EAST
♠ J 9 5 4 2
♡ 9 4
♦ A J 10 4
♣ A 8

SOUTH
♠ A 7
♡ 10 8 7 6 5 3 2
♦ K 5
♣ K 2

The realization that East would need both minor-suit aces for five hearts to succeed was the crucial factor here, and Jim took full advantage of the situation. It turned out that five spades can be made, so even had five hearts gone down, it would not have been a disaster.

The next hand is another that takes into consideration not only the themes from this chapter but some of the earlier ones as well.

```
                    NORTH
                    ♠  K J 9 5
                    ♡  7 3
                    ◇  K 8 7
                    ♣  7 6 5 4


                    SOUTH
                    ♠  8
                    ♡  A K Q J 10 4 2
                    ◇  J 6 3
                    ♣  A 10
```

WEST	NORTH	EAST	SOUTH
1 ♠	Pass	2 ♠	4 ♡
Pass	Pass	Pass	

West leads the club king, you win and draw trumps. West has a singleton and discards a small spade and a small diamond on the second and third round of trumps. You now lead your spade and West plays small. What do you do? Why?

Your thoughts should include the following. Assuming that the correct guess in spades is made, the diamond ace will still have to be found with West. Going back to Chapters Two and Three, West's hand is reconstructed:

West has   the K-Q-(J)-x of clubs
           the diamond ace (assumed)
           the ace or queen of spades

If West has the spade ace, it means East raised one spade to two spades on at best:

♠ Q x x
♥ x x x
♦ Q x x x
♣ x x x

This seems rather thin for a raise. East is more likely to have:

♠ A x x
♥ x x x
♦ Q x x
♣ x x x

The correct play is the jack of spades. Later you hope to enter dummy with the king of diamonds in order to discard some loser on the spade king.

NORTH
♠ K J 9 5
♥ 7 3
♦ K 8 7
♣ 7 6 5 4

WEST
♠ Q 10 7 4 2
♥ 8
♦ A 9 4 2
♣ K Q J

EAST
♠ A 6 3
♥ 9 6 5
♦ Q 10 5
♣ 9 8 3 2

SOUTH
♠ 8
♥ A K Q J 10 4 2
♦ J 6 3
♣ A 10

Quiz

NORTH
♠ 8 2
♡ K J 9 7
◊ A J 4 2
♣ J 10 6

SOUTH
♠ 9 5 3
♡ A Q 10 8 6 4
◊ Q 3
♣ K 5

NORTH	EAST	SOUTH	WEST
Pass	Pass	1 ♡	1 ♠
3 ♡	3 ♠	4 ♡	Pass
Pass	Pass		

West leads the spade king. East plays the queen. West continues with the spade six to East's ten. The club three is returned.

1. Who has what in spades?

2. What are your sure losers?

3. What must happen for you to succeed?

4. How do you "approach" the hand?

5. What is your play?

Answers

NORTH
- ♠ 8 2
- ♡ K J 9 7
- ◇ A J 4 2
- ♣ J 10 6

WEST
- ♠ A K 7 6 4
- ♡ 5
- ◇ K 8 6 5
- ♣ Q 9 4

EAST
- ♠ Q J 10
- ♡ 3 2
- ◇ 10 9 7
- ♣ A 8 7 3 2

SOUTH
- ♠ 9 5 3
- ♡ A Q 10 8 6 4
- ◇ Q 3
- ♣ K 5

West leads the spade king, and East follows with the queen. The spade six is led to East's ten, and East returns the club three.

1. West has the A-K-x-x-x of spades. East has the Q-J-10 of spades.
2. The sure losers are two spades and a club.
3. You must guess clubs, and the diamond king must be with West.
4. You make a wish (CPA) that West has the diamond king.
5. If West has the diamond king, it means East has bid three spades on something like this:

♠ Q J 10	or	♠ Q J 10	or	♠ Q J 10
♡ x		♡ x x		♡ x
◇ 10 x x x		◇ x x x		◇ x x x
♣ A x x x x		♣ Q x x x x		♣ Q x x x x

It seems most reasonable to play East for the club ace and West for the queen.

Quiz

```
NORTH
♠  9 2
♡  Q 5 4
◇  A 8 6 3
♣  A 5 4 2

SOUTH
♠  K Q 10 8 5 3
♡  A 9 2
◇  7 4
♣  K 3
```

WEST	NORTH	EAST	SOUTH
Pass	Pass	Pass	1 ♠
2 ◇	2NT	Pass	4 ♠
Pass	Pass	Pass	

West leads the diamond king, which you take; East follows with the five. The spade two is led to the king, which wins; East plays the six and West the four. Dummy is entered with a club and the spade nine is led. East plays the seven.

1. What does West have in diamonds?

2. What does West have in clubs and hearts?

3. Can you make this hand if East has A-J-x-x of spades?

4. Do you make a wish (CPA), and what is it if you do?

5. What does your hypothesis do for you?

6. What do you play?

Answers

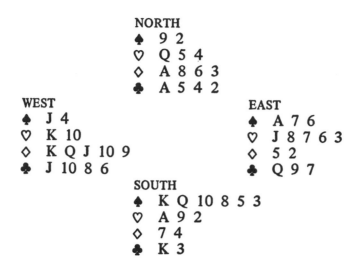

NORTH
♠ 9 2
♡ Q 5 4
◇ A 8 6 3
♣ A 5 4 2

WEST
♠ J 4
♡ K 10
◇ K Q J 10 9
♣ J 10 8 6

EAST
♠ A 7 6
♡ J 8 7 6 3
◇ 5 2
♣ Q 9 7

SOUTH
♠ K Q 10 8 5 3
♡ A 9 2
◇ 7 4
♣ K 3

West's diamond king is taken by the ace. The two of spades goes to the king, getting the six and four. The club three to dummy, and another spade gets the seven from East. Your play.

1. West has K-Q-J-10-x or K-Q-10-9-x. Perhaps he has a sixth diamond.
2. Not clear at this point.
3. No. If East has A-J-x-x of spades you will have to lose two spades, a heart, and a diamond.
4. Wish for West to have the heart king. This will hold your heart losers to one.
5. This hypothesis "gives" West a minimum of 8 points and probably 9 if his diamonds are headed by the king-queen-jack.
6. If you decide West has the heart king, it is clear he is unlikely to have the spade ace too. He would open the bidding. Try the spade king.

Quiz

NORTH
♠ 8 6 4
♡ K Q 2
◇ 8 6 5 3
♣ A K 7

SOUTH
♠ A K J
♡ J 5 4
◇ Q 9 4 2
♣ 9 6 3

EAST	SOUTH	WEST	NORTH
Pass	Pass	Pass	1 ◇
1 ♠	3NT	Pass	Pass
Pass			

So it was late, and you wanted to get home.

West's lead of the heart ten went to East's ace as you played low from dummy. East returned the spade ten.

If you make this you can get away from the idiot partner of yours.

1. Do you think this is likely to be the last hand of the evening?

2. What chances do you have?

3. What tricks do you hope to take?

4. What things in particular must happen to allow you to get those tricks?

5. If the things that *must* happen, do happen, what else will occur?

6. So how do you play?

Answers

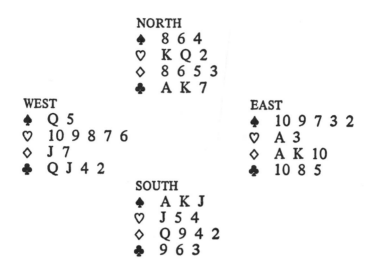

NORTH
♠ 8 6 4
♡ K Q 2
◇ 8 6 5 3
♣ A K 7

WEST
♠ Q 5
♡ 10 9 8 7 6
◇ J 7
♣ Q J 4 2

EAST
♠ 10 9 7 3 2
♡ A 3
◇ A K 10
♣ 10 8 5

SOUTH
♠ A K J
♡ J 5 4
◇ Q 9 4 2
♣ 9 6 3

West led the heart ten to dummy's two and East's ace. The spade ten came back.

1. There is an excellent possibility that you will get to play some more hands.
2. Your chances range from poor to abysmal.
3. You hope to take three spades and two tricks each in hearts, diamonds, and clubs. There is no place for another trick to materialize.
4. To get three spades you will have to find the queen (if possible), and you will need the ace and king of diamonds with East. If West has a diamond honor, there is no way to get two tricks in diamonds. Also, diamonds must divide three-two.
5. If East does have the ace and king of diamonds and the heart ace which you just saw, then can he have the spade queen also? No.
6. You must hope West has the queen doubleton or singleton in spades. If all this comes true, and it is quite a parlay, you are home. But it is the only

way. Then you can lean back and enjoy yourself as East tells West how a spade lead would have beaten you. Life can be so beautiful.

Quiz

NORTH
- ♠ Q 8
- ♡ J 10 3
- ◊ A Q J 2
- ♣ K 9 6 4

SOUTH
- ♠ K 7 6 5 4 3
- ♡ Q 5 2
- ◊ 3
- ♣ A 8 7

SOUTH	WEST	NORTH	EAST
Pass	1 ◊	Pass	2 ◊
2 ♠	Pass	3NT	Pass
4 ♠	Pass	Pass	Pass

West leads the king and ace of hearts, East following with the six and seven. At trick three West shifts to the diamond four.

1.   Can you hold this spade suit to one loser?

2.   What will you do with your club loser?

3.   If East has the ace of spades can you conceivably make four spades?

4.   If West has the king of diamonds can you conceivably make four spades?

    5.   What assumption will you have to make?

    6.   What does the result of this assumption dictate that you do?

Answers

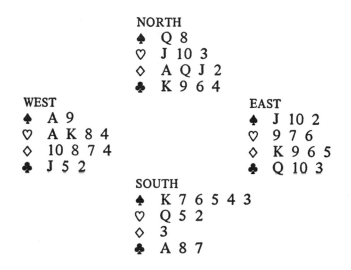

```
                      NORTH
                      ♠ Q 8
                      ♡ J 10 3
                      ◊ A Q J 2
                      ♣ K 9 6 4
WEST                                      EAST
♠ A 9                                     ♠ J 10 2
♡ A K 8 4                                 ♡ 9 7 6
◊ 10 8 7 4                                ◊ K 9 6 5
♣ J 5 2                                   ♣ Q 10 3
                      SOUTH
                      ♠ K 7 6 5 4 3
                      ♡ Q 5 2
                      ◊ 3
                      ♣ A 8 7
```

West leads the king and ace of hearts, East playing the six and seven. West shifts to the diamond four.

    1.   Yes. If West has the ace doubleton of spades you can lead to the queen and duck on the way back (obligatory finesse). Note that if West has the ace singleton or ace tripleton, you must lose two tricks.

    2.   Your club loser must go on the diamond suit. You must guess who has the king.

    3.   If East has the ace of spades you must lose two spade tricks no matter what his holding is. Try it.

    4.   If West has the king of diamonds it is very unlikely that he has the ace of spades also. It would mean

East raised one diamond to two diamonds with a crummy 4 points (at best).

5. If you accept the premise that both the spade ace and the diamond king are unlikely to be with West, then you must assume as follows: West has to have the ace doubleton of spades. Therefore, if I am going to make four spades, I assume it is so. From this I conclude East has the king of diamonds.

6. Play the diamond ace and return the queen. If East does not cover, throw your club loser away. If this is successful you need find West with two spades only (including the ace), and another routine game is in the bag.

Once again a little thought brings a big reward. It is always better to do a little thinking early than a lot of mourning late.

Quiz

```
                NORTH
                ♠  8 3
                ♡  J 10 3
                ◇  A Q J
                ♣  K 9 6 4 3


                SOUTH
                ♠  K Q 7 6 5 4
                ♡  Q 5 2
                ◇  3
                ♣  A 8 7
```

WEST	NORTH	EAST	SOUTH
1 ◇	Pass	2 ◇	2 ♠
Pass	2NT	Pass	3 ♠
Pass	4 ♠	Pass	Pass
Pass			

West leads the king and the ace of hearts. East follows with the six and the seven. West shifts to the diamond ten.

1.   Is this hand familiar?

What other questions do you ask? What are the answers to these questions?

```
                    NORTH
                    ♠  8 3
                    ♡  J 10 3
                    ◇  A Q J
                    ♣  K 9 6 4 3
WEST                                    EAST
♠  10 9                                 ♠  A J 2
♡  A K 8 4                              ♡  9 7 6
◇  K 10 9 4                             ◇  8 7 6 5 2
♣  Q 10 2                               ♣  J 5
                    SOUTH
                    ♠  K Q 7 6 5 4
                    ♡  Q 5 2
                    ◇  3
                    ♣  A 8 7
```

Questions and Answers:

1.   This hand is almost the same as the preceding hand.

2.   Where is the club loser going?

2.   It must go on the diamond suit. You must guess who has the diamond king.

3.   Can four spades make if West has the spade ace?

3.   No. If West has the spade ace you will go down regardless of the remainder of the spade distribution. Try it.

4.   What must I assume?

4.   East has to have the spade ace.

5.   If East has it, what does it indicate about the remainder of the hand?

5.   There are 18 points missing. If East has the ace of spades (assumed) and the diamond king, then West will have opened on a terrible 11 points. West will probably have the king of diamonds.

6.   What is the correct play?

6.   Play the diamond queen and pray.

Quiz

NORTH
♠ A K 10 4
♡ Q 6 5 4 3
◇ K Q
♣ J 2

SOUTH
♠ 9 8 7 6 2
♡ J
◇ J 9
♣ K 8 7 6 4

WEST	NORTH	EAST	SOUTH
1NT	2 ♣	2 ◇	4 ♠
Pass	Pass	Pass	

One notrump equals 16 to 18 points. Two clubs is a conventional response, called the Landy Convention, showing the major suits.

West leads the heart king. East plays the two. West cashes the diamond ace and East plays another two. West now plays the spade three. It is your turn to think. What are your thoughts?

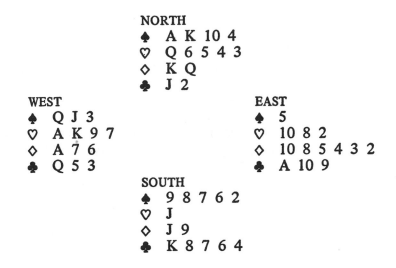

NORTH
♠ A K 10 4
♡ Q 6 5 4 3
◇ K Q
♣ J 2

WEST
♠ Q J 3
♡ A K 9 7
◇ A 7 6
♣ Q 5 3

EAST
♠ 5
♡ 10 8 2
◇ 10 8 5 4 3 2
♣ A 10 9

SOUTH
♠ 9 8 7 6 2
♡ J
◇ J 9
♣ K 8 7 6 4

One notrump equals 16 to 18 points. Two clubs is the majors (Landy Convention). West leads the heart king, the diamond ace, and the spade three.

Questions and Answers:

    1.   What is the range of the one notrump?
        1.   Sixteen to 18 points.
    2.   How many points am I missing?
        2.   Twenty points.

3.   What miracle will be needed to make this?
   3.   I must lose only one club trick and no spades.
4.   How can I lose only one club trick?
   4.   East has the ace of clubs or the singleton queen.
5.   Which one is more likely?
   5.   The club ace. The chances of a singleton queen are quite remote. And East did make a free bid. It is not at all impossible to find the club ace with East.
6.   What does this all mean to me?
   6.   If East has the club ace it will use up 4 of the missing 20 points. West will need the rest.
7.   What is the proper play?
   7.   If West has the 16 points he needs for the one-notrump opening bid, he will have both the queen and jack of spades. It may go against the grain, but the correct play is to play low on the spade lead.

7

Making Your Sixth Sense Work

♠ ♡ ◇ ♣

In the normal play or defense of a hand, every declarer or defender has noticed on occasion a twitch, hitch, tremor, trance, or even a huddle on the part of an opponent. No matter what you call it, there was some abnormality of varying degree in the usual tempo of action.

These "abnormalities" occur in the auction as well as in the play, but for the most part the cause is not as easily ascertained in the bidding as it is in the play, which is difficult enough. In any case, this book is intended to cover various aspects of card play, and with this in mind I will try not to wander into the fantasy world of bidding.

For the rest of this chapter, all giveaway actions will be lumped together under the heading of "Tells" for two reasons: All of these abnormalities "tell" something to the watchful player, and "tell" is much the shortest word available. Some Tells are real and some are not.

How can a Tell not be real? If you saw or felt something, then something happened. But it may or may not have any significance. You will have to learn to differentiate between real Tells and false Tells. How can you do that?

Let's look at an everyday analogy. After a session you have this super hand you played so well, and you want to show it to someone. Fortunately for you, your friend Joe is there and you can bend his ear a bit about your hand. Unfortunately for you, Joe has a hand of his own and he is just as interested in bending your ear about his hand. Inevitably, by mutual unwritten consent you agree to listen to each other's hands. You, being the dominant personality, start first and at the conclusion of your story you look to Joe for approval. But rather than approval, Joe's eyes light up with a fire of enthusiasm and he leans forward and says his first words in five minutes: "I had seven spades to the king-queen-jack. . . ." You realize that he has not heard a word of what you said. He has been in his own world waiting to give you his hand.

It is this frame of mind in which so many defenders find themselves when you lead a card. They were not paying attention, and their motor reflexes to get to the card they wish to play and muddled by the effort to get their minds on the proper suit, as well as their hand on the proper card. You must realize that some Tells like this are involuntary and have nothing to do with what cards are held.

Unfortunately some people have learned to imitate this particular Tell, and there are rumors out that they have been known to perform this particular Tell on purpose. This is unfortunate, as it goes against the spirit of the game.

These people think that by doing this they may be able to mislead a watchful declarer. Some players approach bridge like a poker game: no holds barred, with bluffs and counterbluffs, etc. They are merely misinformed as to the proprieties of the game and would be very honestly unhappy to be informed their actions were illegal. Some of the others, sad to say, seem to feel that this tricky act of theirs helps them win, and they do it in full understanding of the laws of bridge.

You might doubt that these people actually gain any advantage from their performances. But sadly they do. It is rarely successful in good competition however. Any declarer who has been stung once or twice will begin to note when he has been misled by a Tell; and if he cannot identify with the Tell, then perhaps he can remember the person who did it to him.

If it is going to happen, it will be necessary for you to see the difference. Let's go back to our friend Joe.

Remember Joe? He was not paying attention to you. He was paying attention to nothing. If a pretty redhead walked by, you would have seen that he was interested in something. But surely not your bridge hand. In the same way our actor seems to be interested in something, but for some reason it is not bridge.

In some cases it is not important to be able to tell the difference.

If you are looking for a specific card, such as a queen, the actor does not have it. Furthermore, the lethargic player does not have it either. When you make your play against this kind of defender, the one who has the critical card is more likely to recover quickly than the one who does not have it.

This does not mean, however, that whenever someone flickers you should assume he does not have the crucial card.

Not at all. What you have to do is learn the difference between all of the above and a real, live, honest huddle. After all, the defenders do frequently have a problem, and sometimes they are placed in a position of having to decide the answer in split seconds. Then the huddle may be just momentary, but a huddle nonetheless.

Here is the difference. Let's go back to Joe again. As you are giving him your hand, his eyes are again filling with enthusiasm; but this time when you finish he leans forward and says, "Wow! A real-life transfer repeating criss-cross double squeeze. Show me again!" This time you know he is really interested in what you are saying. The same way with your defenders. The line is very fine, but if you try to observe all the Tells with which you are abundantly surrounded, in time the differences will become apparent.

PLAYER TYPES

Let's digress just for a second and look at the players first. Players are divided into two groups. One group is quiet and secure and all cards come from this group in a rather even tempo. There are no fast cards or slow cards. Watch out for these people. They are frequently better than they may first appear. Of course, they may just be new players and are merely nervous. Nervous players usually play slowly and, until their nervousness leaves them, badly.

The other group consists of the activists. These are the people who squirm and fidget and generally cannot sit still. Almost all of the actors fall into this group. Luckily, very few squirmers are actors.

When you do actually run into a genuine actor, it may be possible to identify him. A couple of tricks used by the actor are:

(1) Without actually detaching a card, but by rapidly moving the free hand among his cards and apparently clutching now and then at one or *some* of them, the actor may appear to be having a problem.

(2) He may lurch forward as if to inspect the dummy before he plays. This one is tricky. Many players have an honest concern with what is in the dummy. Here the key is the amount of interest being generated by the player. (Is Joe interested in the redhead or your story?)

Sometimes you can tell if it is an actor who is giving you the business by playing with his cards rather than a slow or even awkward player who is in a state of honest confusion.

Most actors do not have enough gall to take a card and make a major move to detach it before putting it back in favor of some other card, which may or may not in its turn be a repeat performance of the first card. These people sort of flirt from card to card before beginning to detach and play their "final choice." When you are missing only three cards in a suit, always beware of the man who seems to have six or seven choices before following suit. Beware also of the man who, when faced with the apparent option of taking or not taking a trick (he could play his hypothetical high card or one of two or three small cards), appears to have oodles of pleasant choices.

Compare this with the player who really has a problem.

For starters, this player is less likely to begin to play a card until he intends to play it. This player, when playing that card, may even appear slightly in doubt after having removed it from his hand, and may give the impression that he would like to play something else. Very possibly, in fact, he will replace it in favor of another card.

This is something the actor will not do. In most situations the actor is doing his thing when he has no problem, so his performance is concluded when he finally gets a grip on a card and starts to play it. Remember that he will not, in fact, have any real live choices, and he is unlikely to change cards once it is on the way.

OTHER SYMPTOMS OF THE PLAYER
WITH A PROBLEM

You have seen this one before. "One spade" by you, and a minute later your LHO comes out of a stupor with, "Did you bid something?" Sometimes this man is trying to hide a problem. Sometimes he did not hear your bid.

If, after the "Did you bid something?" speech, you inform him that you had bid one spade and the man then makes a fast bid, it probably means he has spent that minute deciding what to do over one spade. On the other hand, if he takes a few seconds to do something then he likely did not hear your bid.

This applies as well in the play. It is very hard not to notice that someone has played a card. The person who, after much delay, is informed that it is his play and who then plays quickly, has almost surely been thinking in the meantime. Most people who are sufficiently unalert to see that it is their play, are unlikely to be instantly prepared when they are duly informed. When someone says in the middle of a crucial trick that they "are working out the whole hand" or, instead, they take a few minutes to think and then follow suit in a noncritical situation, you can be sure they are anticipating a later problem. Anticipate with them. They are helping you.

The upshot of all this is that you are looking for some form of hesitation, and you leave it up to your judgment to decide what it means.

THE SHOTGUN

Certainly any deviation from the normal tempo has some meaning, but not all deviations are of the slow variety. Frequently you are treated to a "shotgun."

A shotgun is a card that has been played with a degree of haste out of all proportion to the normal tempo of the player.

Is this like the person who has a singleton deuce and, when his partner leads the ace, allows his emotions to overcome everything else, and in an effort to get partner to continue the suit flings the deuce with considerable vim and vigor—and not infrequently a heavy thump in addition—out onto the table?

No. Not at all, although you may feel as though you had been shot. The situation referred to here is the common one in which you have come down to trick ten or eleven and, for example, you have to lead toward the king-jack in dummy. To make your contract you must guess correctly. You know this, and most certainly your opponents do also. The player on your left has the ace and he has been watching you for the duration of the hand as you performed various bridge gymnastics in an effort to get some clear idea as to this suit. Perhaps you have succeeded and perhaps you have not, but when you finally lead that suit, he is ready. No hesitation on his part. No sir. For ten minutes this moment has been approaching, and he has been anticipating it every second of that time. At last! You reach for that card. You detach it. Still muddled in thought and finally, no longer able to postpone the decision, you fling it out for inspection. But now a funny thing happens. Your card, before it can complete its first bounce, has company. There is another card out there. That card is clearly not yours, not the dummy's, and it is not the ace. It is a little one belonging to that nervous player on your left. He has gotten so worked up to not hesitating with that ace that normal play is out of the question.

This does not mean, however, that every fast play is unusual.

Many people play very fast all the time. The "shotgun" situation usually comes about in certain stereotyped situations.

These include, among others, the situation like the preceding one. Additionally is the player who has a king behind dummy's A-Q-J-10 and refused the first trick when you took a finesse. He may exhibit some signs in this direction. Certainly if he had only the doubleton king behind the A-Q-J-10 he might show signs of wear.

Usually the shotgun makes its appearance at times when there is some tension in the air. Certainly when declarer was making his guess in the above hand, there was some reason for a less-than-relaxed atmosphere.

You *may* even be able to test a player to get his "nervous rating."

The defender who had the ace in the earlier hand and who had all that time to get ready may be feeling some side effects. If you think of it, you might take a sip of some cold drink before playing and then offer him some. His reaction may tell you something. Perhaps he will have an exceedingly dry mouth or perhaps he will not even answer you, or perhaps both. Perhaps he may try to answer you and cannot get the words out. Hmmm.

Of course, if you do not have a drink, you can play like anybody else. Certainly not everyone is going to be offering their opponents drinks every time they have to guess a queen. But there is one thing you should always notice whenever a "shotgun" appears.

This particular point is intended to help you decide if you are seeing a shotgun or just a normal very fast card. You will remember that the person playing a card in one of these situations has frequently been getting himself worked up into some kind of lather. The last thing he wants is to draw attention to himself, and he is striving for normalcy in his play tempo. A person who is shotgunning his card will probably not play it firmly. No slap, no thump, and very likely it will be stuck to the fingertips. The person who normally plays a card quickly is just following his or her natural rhythm, and the card may well bounce a bit. But the hand that plays it is quickly disengaged from the card and will not long be around the table. Not so the nervous shotgunner. Afraid to do anything fast now (he is already feeling embarrassed that his play tempo was not what he had in mind), his hand may hover on or near the card before a slow withdrawal ensues.

The summation of all of this seems to indicate that the man who flickers hasn't the missing card unless he does have it. This is correct and is not at all the same as the very common misinterpretation which reads, "The man who flickers has the missing card unless he doesn't have it." The man who does not understand the difference has inevitably lost to more queens than the man who does understand. All you have to do when someone hesitates is to judge what kind of interest that person is demonstrating. The shotgunner seems fairly easy—he is surely an interested participant and he is probably the easiest to spot.

The others will be a little harder to identify. Only through practice on your part in noticing any Tells, and then looking to see what the situation was, will you acquire the ability to "feel" your way about the table.

Unfortunately, all of the preceding discussion does not totally cover this area at all. In fact, it is very much further complicated by something not yet delved into.

WHAT CARD AM I LOOKING FOR?

Look at the two card combinations below. What are the differences between these two suits. South leads the three toward the dummy. You are defending in the West seat.

	NORTH			NORTH	
	K J 10			K J 10	
WEST		EAST	WEST		EAST
Q 5 4		?	Q 5 4		?
	SOUTH			SOUTH	
	?			?	
	3 is led			3 is led	

There may appear to be no difference between these two situations. But that is the result of insufficient depth of analysis. A glass of water is worth far more to a man lost in the desert than is the same glass to a man in the comfort of his own home.

By putting these cards in different contexts, the differences will be seen. And the "What card am I looking for?" question will acquire some meaning.

I showed you a position as a defender. Here are some of the varying situations declarer may be facing.

Declarer is in six notrump.

In this setting South needs to guess whether to play the king or the jack of spades. He needs just one trick in the spade suit.

NORTH
♠ K J 10
♡ A Q 2
◇ K 3 2
♣ K 7 6 5

SOUTH
♠ 6 3
♡ K J 10 4
◇ A Q J
♣ A Q J 10

Declarer is in four spades.

In this setup South needs again to guess whether to play the king or the jack of spades. But rather than being concerned with winning one trick, he is trying not to lose two.

NORTH
♠ K J 10
♡ K 3 2
◇ Q 3
♣ 8 7 6 5 4

SOUTH
♠ 9 8 7 6 3 2
♡ A Q J
◇ J 3
♣ A K

Declarer is in three notrump this time. He received a diamond lead and came to his hand with a club.

Now he needs to guess whether to play the spade king and then the jack for a finesse the other way, or whether to play to the jack immediately.

NORTH
♠ K J 10
♡ A 4 3 2
◇ A 4
♣ 6 4 3 2

SOUTH
♠ A 9 8 3
♡ K 7 6
◇ 6 3
♣ A K 7 5

Here you have a grand slam in seven spades.

Quite aside from the other problems at hand, declarer would be happy to guess the spades.

NORTH
♠ K J 10
♡ A Q
◇ K 2
♣ K 8 6 4 3 2

SOUTH
♠ A 9 8 7 6 3
♡ K 2
◇ A 5 4 3
♣ A

And for the last case, the contract is four hearts. The defense led a heart.

A spade trick is needed to take care of the club loser.

NORTH
♠ K J 10
♡ A 8 6 4 2
◇ 8 3
♣ K 8 7

SOUTH
♠ 3
♡ K Q J 5 3
◇ 10 9 5 2
♣ A 6 3

Do these examples help you see what I'm driving at?

The point being made is that these situations, although very much alike when the cards you can see are taken in isolation, are actually quite unrelated.

Notice also that the "What card am I looking for?" question can be reworded for the defender to "What card is *he* looking for?"

In each of the situations given earlier, the declarer is going to play that suit one way or the other, and his reasons or considerations are not at all the same in any of the five cases. There are a million situations like that one. What would you be thinking in those cases as a declarer or a defender?

In all five cases, when you play the three of spades there is going to be a different level of excitement in the air. On that six-notrump hand, by the time you get around to that spade guess everyone will know what the problem is. It is possible you'll get a shotgun.

And in the second hand where you were in four spades, the West player holding Q-5-4 probably would not be too concerned. If spades had been bid strongly, West would probably not know there was a problem similar to the first one. There would be very little tension around when the spade three was led. Likewise on the three-notrump hand. But the grand-slam hand will certainly be a nervous one. Declarer will not be rushing to get a trump on the table. Even though he knows he is going to lead one sooner or later, he is going to think about it first; and when he does, there will be an atmosphere of anticipation about the table. Especially if spades are Q-5-4 in the West hand.

What do you think about the four-heart hand? Anything going on there?

```
                NORTH
                ♠  K J 10
                ♡  A 8 6 4 2
                ◊  8 3
                ♣  K 8 7

                SOUTH
                ♠  3
                ♡  K Q J 5 3
                ◊  10 9 5 2
                ♣  A 6 3
```

Possibly—it would depend on the bidding. If spades had been bid by the defense, and declarer was known to have a singleton, then there would be that feel in the air when the three was led. So it is possible you might well see the same player in that West seat holding exactly the same cards produce clearly different mannerisms when the spade three is led in the five contracts.

You probably would not get five variations, but it would not be at all surprising to see *some* variations. And do not lose sight of the fact that these things are more the exception than the rule. Remember, your problem is only to identify the action. If the person is just in a thoughtless muddle, you have to recognize that and then make your normal guess. If he has an honest problem, it is to your benefit. And if he is an actor, then you can again benefit if you are sure of your estimation of the person.

In the above situations the actor may perform differently depending on his estimation of what card or cards you are missing. The hand you played in six notrump, for instance, might find him hitching with the queen but not with the ace. How about that for a double-cross? You would hardly expect an opponent to have a problem on the three-notrump hand, and it is possible you might get a baby shotgun on the seven-spade hand by the man with Q-5-4 of trumps.

I may have misused the term "baby shotgun," but it seems to describe the circumstance of a . . . well . . . maybe a quickish nervous card played oh so silently. I saw a man once in this very situation play his card and then lean back in his chair and quietly cough once. . . .

In the last few pages you learned that everything is not necessarily as it appears. You saw that what looked like exactly identical card combinations were not identical at all. They were treated in a completely different fashion according to the environment. A different contract or a different auction might cause some variations in the proceedings. Now let's take two groups of card combinations that at first glance seem to fall into the area of close brothers, if not twins. From a declarer's point of view, look at these various pairs of combinations and decide what they have in common. Consider them in light of the preceding discussion on "What card am I looking for?"

Here are the combinations:

	1(a)	NORTH	1(b)	NORTH
		A 9 8		A Q J
		SOUTH		SOUTH
		Q J 10		10 9 8

2(a)   NORTH
K 9 8

SOUTH
J 10

2(b)   NORTH
K J 10

SOUTH
9 8

3(a)   NORTH
K Q 7

SOUTH
10 9 8

3(b)   NORTH
K Q 10

SOUTH
9 8 7

4(a)   NORTH
K 9 2

SOUTH
J 10

4(b)   NORTH
K 10 9

SOUTH
J 2

4(c)   NORTH
K J 10

SOUTH
9 2

Well, what feelings do you have for these situations? Are the three pairings alike or not alike?

1(a)   NORTH
A 9 8

SOUTH
Q J 10

1(b)   NORTH
A Q J

SOUTH
10 9 8

It seems to me that they look rather similar. In the first pair, for instance, I will lead the queen in (a). If the king is with West I make three tricks. If East has the king I will make two. In (b) I lead to the queen, and if it wins I will later lead to the jack. I will make three or two tricks as in (a), depending on the location of the king. What is the difference?

I cannot really define it. But it seems to me that in (a), when the queen is led, our old friend tension may be about if West has the king. If East has the king there will be no emotion in the air and the defense will be quite relaxed.

There is one small additional consideration: the case when East has the singleton king. You may notice an even more acute degree of suspense than might be expected. This is not to suggest, however, that you try to drop the king.

No. Only very rarely should you try something like this. And for a good reason.

This is the reason, and every now and then when I ignore it, I usually pay for it: While it is usually very easy to note some change in the normal atmosphere at the table, it is *extremely difficult to measure*. Do not try to estimate the degree of change. Remember, if West has the king, there may be some feelings radiating from him. He may be wondering if perhaps he should have covered the queen. East may be rooting for you to go up with the ace trying to drop a king that is not there to drop. It is much too difficult to tell the difference in this atmosphere from the one that prevails when East has the king bare.

This does not mean you should not go against percentages.

In the case being discussed, you probably should not try to drop that king because your play would be incredibly against the odds. Only in the event that you had some major reason, such as was covered in the earlier chapters of this book, should you go wildly against percentages. The time you should be paying attention to your sixth sense is when you are involved in what appears to be even or almost even-money decisions. Your "feel" may cause you to attempt to drop a doubleton queen when missing five cards. But short of someone spilling his cards face up on the table, it is difficult to imagine a situation where you would go so much against the odds as to try to drop a king missing seven cards in a suit.

2(a)   NORTH   What do you think of case 2(a) and
        K 9 8   (b)? Is this just another example of the
                         tension bit?
        SOUTH
        J 10

2(b)   NORTH
       K J 10

       SOUTH
       9 8

Yes. But why does this occur? And what case, (a) or (b), is likely to be easier to guess? Why?

In case (a), if West has the ace he has to decide whether or not to take it, and if he has the queen he has to decide whether or not to cover if the jack has been led. It is evident that West will frequently have a problem.

And in (b)? In this case, when the eight or nine is led West will have to decide if he should take his ace—if he has it. Any West who has the queen only will not be concerned with whether or not he ought to play the queen. In (a), West might hope to gain a trick by covering the jack with the queen, but in (b) it is clear that nothing can be gained by inserting the queen. So West will not think about it unless he is a very professional actor. The trick is to play your cards in such a way as to be able to guess correctly what the defenders are thinking about. Look carefully at the next pair of combinations.

3(a)   NORTH
       K Q 7

       SOUTH
       10 9 8

In the third set of hands, if you lead the eight to the king in (a) and it wins, you can come back and lead the nine. It may look to West that you are going to play the queen if he, West, has the ace and does not play it. It may seem that you are only interested in the location of the ace.

3(b)   NORTH
       K Q 10

       SOUTH
       9 8 7

But in (b), West can see clearly that the location of the jack is important. West is more likely to play low with the ace in (b) than (a) on the second round of the suit. If West thinks on the second round of the suit when you lead the nine in (a), he probably has the ace. However, if you lead the ten at trick two of the suit in (a), you gave West two possible problems. In light of the above, how do you play to play 4(a), (b), and (c) assuming your contract depends on losing one trick only?

In all three cases you should lead low toward the dummy. If in 4(a) or 4(b) you lead the jack, then West may have a problem—but you will not know if he was wondering what to do with the ace or the queen.

One last common Tell available to you which is about as sure a Tell as you will ever get. This is your trump suit:

NORTH
A 10 9 8

SOUTH
K J 7 4 2

You led the ace, on which all followed, and continued with the ten, East producing the remaining small card. Do you finesse or play for the drop? While you are thinking about this, you observe that West has detached or is beginning to detach a card. How does this influence you, if at all?

If the solution of this Tell is not immediately clear to you, ask yourself how you would play if you were the defender on declarer's left—

(1) With the trump queen. (2) Without the trump queen, *i.e.,* with an original singleton trump.

In case one, would you be pulling out the queen in anticipation of playing it or would you be clutching your cards firmly so as to prevent declarer spotting the queen in your hand?

In case two, having no problem now, might you not, in a moment of weakness, begin to detach some nonessential card from some other suit?

This particular Tell says you should finesse.

SUMMARY

The first problem you have is to identify what kind of Tell is being made if one occurs. You have to guess if it is real, accidental, or fake. For the most part you should concentrate only on what seem to be real Tells, and *ignore* the rest. These include the shotgun, which is a card played extremely fast.

Next you have to consider the different kind of problems the defense may have. You must recognize that various problems which appear to be twins or look-alikes may, as far as the defense is concerned, be very different. If possible, try to conceal the problem from the defenders.

The only point to be emphasized is that you should *ignore* any Tell that you cannot identify as being for real. There are too many accidental hesitations as well as the phony intentional ones to work out all of them.

Index

50 HIGHLY-RECOMMENDED TITLES

**CALL TOLL FREE 1-800-274-2221
IN THE U.S. & CANADA TO ORDER ANY OF
THEM OR TO REQUEST OUR
FULL-COLOR 64 PAGE CATALOG OF
ALL BRIDGE BOOKS IN PRINT,
SUPPLIES AND GIFTS.**

Prices subject to change without notice.

DEFENSE
#0520 Blackwood-Complete Book of Opening Leads 17.95
#3030 Ewen-Opening Leads 15.95
#0104 Stewart-Baron-The Bridge Book 4 .... 7.95
#0631 Lawrence-Dynamic Defense 11.95
#1200 Woolsey-Modern Defensive Signalling 4.95

FOR INTERMEDIATE PLAYERS
#2120 Kantar-Complete Defensive Bridge 20.00
#3015 Root-Commonsense Bidding 15.00
#0630 Lawrence-Card Combinations 12.95
#0102 Stewart-Baron-The Bridge Book 2 .... 9.95
#1102 Silverman-Intermediate Bridge Five
      Card Major Student Text 4.95
#0575 Lampert-The Fun Way to Advanced Bridge 11.95
#0633 Lawrence-How to Read Your Opponents' Cards 9.95
#3672 Truscott-Bid Better, Play Better 11.00
#1765 Lawrence-Judgment at Bridge 9.95

PLAY OF THE HAND
#2150 Kantar-Test your Bridge Play, Vol. 1 .... 10.00
#3675 Watson-Watson's Classic Book on
      the Play of the Hand 12.00
#1932 Mollo-Gardener-Card Play Technique 12.95
#3009 Root-How to Play a Bridge Hand 12.00
#1104 Silverman-Play of the Hand as
      Declarer and Defender 4.95
#2175 Truscott-Winning Declarer Play 10.00
#3803 Sydnor-Bridge Made Easy Book 3 .... 6.00

CONVENTIONS
#2115 Kantar-Bridge Conventions 10.00
#0610 Kearse-Bridge Conventions Complete 29.95
#3011 Root-Pavlicek-Modern Bridge Conventions 15.00
#0240 Championship Bridge Series (All 36) 25.95

DUPLICATE STRATEGY
#1600 Klinger-50 Winning Duplicate Tips 12.95
#2260 Sheinwold-Duplicate Bridge 3.95

FOR ALL PLAYERS
#3889 Darvas & de V. Hart-Right Through The Pack 14.95
#0790 Simon: Why You Lose at Bridge 11.95
#4850 Encyclopedia of Bridge, Official (ACBL) 39.95

Andersen THE LEBENSOHL CONVENTION COMPLETE .... $ 6.95
Baron THE BRIDGE PLAYER'S DICTIONARY $19.95
Bergen BETTER BIDDING WITH BERGEN,
    Vol. I, Uncontested Auctions $11.95
Bergen BETTER BIDDING WITH BERGEN,
    Vol. II, Competitive Auctions .... $ 9.95
Blackwood COMPLETE BOOK OF OPENING LEADS $17.95
Blackwood-Hanson PLAY FUNDAMENTALS .... $ 6.95
Boeder THINKING ABOUT IMPS $12.95
Bruno-Hardy 2 OVER 1 GAME FORCE: AN INTRODUCTION .... $ 9.95
Darvas & De V. Hart RIGHT THROUGH THE PACK $12.95
DeSerpa THE MEXICAN CONTRACT .... $ 5.95
Eber & Freeman HAVE I GOT A STORY FOR YOU .... $ 7.95
Feldheim FIVE CARD MAJOR BIDDING IN
    CONTRACT BRIDGE $12.95
Flannery THE FLANNERY 2 DIAMOND OPENING .... $ 7.95
Goldman ACES SCIENTIFIC .... $ 9.95
Goldman WINNERS AND LOSERS AT THE
    BRIDGE TABLE .... $ 3.95
Groner DUPLICATE BRIDGE DIRECTION $14.95
Hardy
    COMPETITIVE BIDDING WITH TWO SUITED HANDS .... $ 9.95
    TWO-OVER-ONE GAME FORCE $14.95
    TWO-OVER-ONE GAME FORCE QUIZ BOOK $11.95
Harris BRIDGE DIRECTOR'S COMPANION (3rd Edition) $19.95
Kay COMPLETE BOOK OF DUPLICATE BRIDGE $14.95
Kearse BRIDGE CONVENTIONS COMPLETE $29.95
Kelsey COUNTDOWN TO BETTER BRIDGE .... $ 9.95
Kelsey THE TRICKY GAME $11.95
Lampert THE FUN WAY TO ADVANCED BRIDGE $11.95
Lawrence
    CARD COMBINATIONS $12.95
    COMPLETE BOOK ON BALANCING $11.95
    COMPLETE BOOK ON OVERCALLS $11.95
    DYNAMIC DEFENSE $11.95
    FALSECARDS .... $ 9.95
    HAND EVALUATION $11.95
    HOW TO READ YOUR OPPONENTS' CARDS $11.95
    JUDGMENT AT BRIDGE .... $ 9.95
    PARTNERSHIP UNDERSTANDINGS .... $ 4.95
    PLAY BRIDGE WITH MIKE LAWRENCE $11.95
    PLAY SWISS TEAMS WITH MIKE LAWRENCE .... $ 7.95
    WORKBOOK ON THE TWO OVER ONE SYSTEM $11.95

Lawrence & Hanson WINNING BRIDGE INTANGIBLES .... $ 4.95
Lipkin INVITATION TO ANNIHILATION .... $ 8.95
Michaels & Cohen 4-3-2-1 MANUAL .... $ 2.95
Penick BEGINNING BRIDGE COMPLETE .... $ 9.95
Penick BEGINNING BRIDGE QUIZZES .... $ 6.95
Powell TICKETS TO THE DEVIL .... $ 5.95
Reese & Hoffman PLAY IT AGAIN, SAM .... $ 7.95
Rosenkranz
      BRIDGE: THE BIDDER'S GAME $12.95
      TIPS FOR TOPS .... $ 9.95
      MORE TIPS FOR TOPS .... $ 9.95
      TRUMP LEADS .... $ 7.95
      OUR MAN GODFREY $10.95
Rosenkranz & Alder BID TO WIN, PLAY FOR PLEASURE $11.95
Rosenkranz & Truscott BIDDING ON TARGET $10.95
Silverman
      ELEMENTARY BRIDGE FIVE CARD MAJOR STUDENT TEXT .... $ 4.95
      INTERMEDIATE BRIDGE FIVE CARD MAJOR STUDENT TEXT .... $ 4.95
      ADVANCED & DUPLICATE BRIDGE STUDENT TEXT .... $ 4.95
      PLAY OF THE HAND AS DECLARER
      & DEFENDER STUDENT TEXT .... $ 4.95
Simon
      CUT FOR PARTNERS .... $ 9.95
      WHY YOU LOSE AT BRIDGE $11.95
Stewart & Baron
      THE BRIDGE BOOK, Vol. 1, Beginning .... $ 9.95
      THE BRIDGE BOOK, Vol. 2, Intermediate .... $ 9.95
      THE BRIDGE BOOK, Vol. 3, Advanced .... $ 9.95
      THE BRIDGE BOOK, Vol. 4, Defense .... $ 7.95
Thomas SHERLOCK HOLMES, BRIDGE DETECTIVE .... $ 9.95
Von Elsner
      CRUISE BRIDGE .... $ 5.95
      EVERYTHING JAKE WITH ME .... $ 5.95
      THE BEST OF JAKE WINKMAN .... $ 5.95
      THE JAKE OF HEARTS .... $ 5.95
Woolsey
      MATCHPOINTS $14.95
      MODERN DEFENSIVE SIGNALLING .... $ 4.95
      PARTNERSHIP DEFENSE $12.95
World Bridge Federation APPEALS COMMITTEE DECISIONS
      from the 1994 NEC WORLD CHAMPIONSHIPS .... $ 9.95